WALKS FROM
THE WELSH HIGHLAND RAILWAY
PART 2

Walks from
The Welsh Highland Railway

Part 2:
Rhyd-ddu to Porthmadog

Dave Salter and Dave Worrall

ISBN: 978-1-84524-135-3

First published in 2009 by
Llygad Gwalch
Llwyndyrys, Pwllheli LL53 6NG
email: llyfrau@carreg-gwalch.com
internet: www.carreg-gwalch.com

Dedicated with admiration,
to the slate quarrymen of Gwynedd:
skillful in their work;
fervent for their culture;
fearless for their rights;
tender in their care for each other

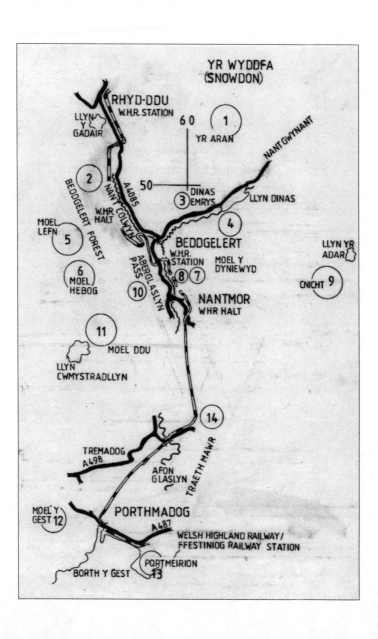

Contents

Introduction

It is now over 4 years since the first book in this series was published. When Volume I came out we were of the opinion that it wouldn't be long before the railway was extended to Porthmadog. So it was with concern and expectation that we observed the dreadfully slow progress that was being made. From the moment the rail track had reached Rhyd-ddu we would check on the progress that the engineers were making in pushing the route through to Porthmadog. Clearly the Aberglaslyn pass with its bridges and tunnels must have provided an engineering nightmare for the builders and of course the necessity to re-instate the Fisherman's path.

The planning permission granted to the Welsh Highland Railway stated that it was not possible to open an intermediate terminus in Beddgelert, so the line had to be opened in one go from Rhyd-ddu to Porthmadog. Also for a period of time it wasn't clear whether a station or halt would be opened at Nantmor. Thankfully these issues have now been resolved and there will be halts in the Beddgelert Forest, Beddgelert itself, Nantmor and Porthmadog. (Although at the time of writing the Nantmor halt had not been started. Thankfully the option of returning via the Fisherman's Path still makes all the walks feasible.) The location of these halts has made a difference to the walks we were able to include in the book if they were to stay true to the concept of people being able to walk from one station to the next.

The walks included in the book have been chosen to provide a variety of experiences. From each station there will be a walk, which is easy to achieve and provides a pleasant outing for a family group or those who do not often get out into the hills. They also provide a good alternative to going on the high tops when the weather is poor. Indeed we have always been of the opinion that there is little point expending the energy to get onto the high tops if you're not able to see anything or the weather makes the experience thoroughly unpleasant.

Other walks take in lesser tops, which provide interesting alternative views and are reasonably challenging. They also tend to be less frequented than the well-known mountains. Finally there are those walks, which provide a high degree of challenge and take in high mountain tops in the area. Save them for days when the weather permits views from the summits, there is nothing more frustrating than a challenging walk to a top that is then shrouded in mist. These walks in the high mountains can be long and remote, requiring good navigational skills and competence. All in all, the variety of routes should cater for the needs of all those who find themselves using the Welsh Highland Railway and wishing to take a walk in the magnificent countryside.

Our advice has always been to start from the station which will be the end of you walk. Then take the train to the start of the walk; this will give you the time to stop as many times as you wish along the way and fully enjoy your surroundings. This way around you will avoid any panic, which may arise when you begin to wonder if you will make it to the station in time to catch the last train!

All the directions are given from an imaginary position just before you reach the next instruction. When we state L or R this generally means at 90 degrees to your last direction of travel, similarly ½ L or R generally means at 45 degrees to your last direction of travel.

During the process we have found much out about the area, which we did not know before. For us it has been a fascinating journey discovering this quiet backwater of Snowdonia. On many of our walks we saw few people, particularly in comparison to other honey pots in the area. For us the quietness is a bonus. So go and enjoy this beautiful part of Snowdonia and ride on one of the most scenic little railways that you will find in the whole of the UK.

Dave Salter
Dave Worrall

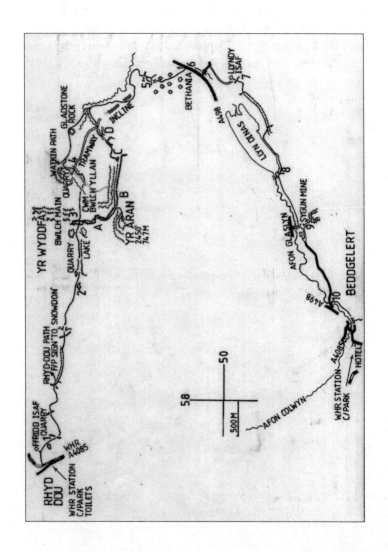

1. Rhyd-ddu to Beddgelert
via Cwm Llan

Maps: 1:50,000 OS Landranger sheet 115 Snowdon/Yr Wyddfa
(Caernarfon) or 1:25,000 OS Explorer sheet OL17 Snowdon/Yr
Wyddfa.

Distance: 8 Miles/ 12.8 Kilometres.

Height gained: 1046ft/319metres (from Rhyd-ddu). For those
wishing to ascend Yr Aran height gained is 1824 ft/ 556 metres
(from Rhyd-ddu).

Duration: 5 hours (Allow an extra 45 minutes + to visit Yr Aran).

Terrain: Good quarry tracks, a steep shale footpath exists during
the descent from Bwlch Cwm Llan. Can be wet underfoot close to
Llyn Dinas.

Stations/Halt: Rhyd-ddu and Beddgelert.

Car Park: Located at the south end of Rhyd-ddu (station) on
A4085 grid reference SH571525 and Beddgelert (behind Royal
Goat Hotel) on the A498 south of the village centre grid reference
SH588481. Both these car parks are Pay and Display.

This pleasant excursion samples the delights of the area to the full.
During the walk you will enjoy views into the spectacular cwms of
Cwm Llan and Cwm Tregalan. If energy and time permits you can
also ascend to the summit of Yr Aran. The "Watkin Path" to the
summit of Snowdon from the Hafod y Llan quarry is also a
possibility given sufficient time, although better routes to the
summit of Snowdon exist.

The path departs from the Rhyd-ddu station, being the original
terminus of the North Wales Narrow Gauge Railway. Originally this

13

stop was known as the Snowdon Station and later re-titled the South Snowdon Station. The terminus opened on 14th May 1881 and was used for the supply of goods and materials to the nearby quarries. It was also used to transport dressed slates from these quarries back to Dinas, close to Caernarfon. From here the slate was loaded onto the more substantial rolling stock of the L&NWR. Rhyd-ddu station was also able to boast the operation of a charabanc service to the village of Beddgelert.

Unfortunately on the 31st of October 1916, all passenger services to this terminus ceased. Under the guise of the Welsh Highland Light Railway and with the backing of the local authorities, the line to South Snowdon was reopened to passengers on 31st July 1922. In the following year, on the 1st of June, a connecting rail service through to Porthmadog commenced. Unfortunately this service was unreliable and intermittent. Consequently it resulted in the closure of the passenger service in 1936 and final closure to freight in 1937.

The South Snowdon station fell into disrepair, partly due to the ravages of the harsh mountain weather in the area and would have become a derelict wreck. However, on 18th of August 2003, after much hard work by the Welsh Highland Railway and with a further delay of nearly four months in 2001 due to the Foot and Mouth epidemic, the Snowdon South terminus and line was reopened to the public.

The path at first follows the confusingly named Beddgelert path towards Yr Wyddfa's summit. Later the path passes close to a small round tower which was the magazine for the storage of explosives for the near by Ffridd quarry. Continue on past the kissing gate, which leads up to Yr Wyddfa and up to the Bwlch Cwm Llan Quarry. The Bwlch Cwm Llan Quarry was opened in the 1840's but the returns from what appears to be such a considerable effort was found to be very modest.

What a difference the current views must have been from the views in the 5th century when Arthur, King of the Britons (the early Welsh), fought a running battle with Mordred. Arthur's Knights forced Mordred and his Saxon army over into Cwm Llan and up into Cwm Tregalan. Mordred's troops were to make a defiant stand at Bwlch y Saethau (pass of the arrows). It was in this battle that the evil Mordred dealt Arthur a lethal blow. As he does so, Arthur strikes Mordred down with Excalibur. Mordred dies screaming whilst Arthur waits quietly for his own death. Mordred's defeated army fled from Arthur's victorious knights over Bwlch Ciliau (Pass of Retreat).

Sir Bedevere carried the mortally wounded Arthur down to the shores of Llyn Llydaw and laid him down. He was then ordered by his King to cast Excalibur into the lake. Three times he went to the waters edge to cast the sword out and twice he was unable to do so. On his return to Arthur, he was asked if his request had been carried out and what did Bedevere see, the reply was nothing. On the third occasion Bedevere threw the sword into the lake and an arm rose to the surface of the lake to grasp Excalibar. The arm waved the sword three times and disappeared. On hearing this Arthur was content and lay quietly. Then through Llydaw's mist came a black boat paddled by three ladies. They took the King into the boat and ferried him back into the mist. With Arthur now returned to Avalon, Bedevere gathered Arthur's Knights and led them to one of the many caves on Lliwedd's steep flanks where they sleep until it is again time to rise and free the people of Britain.

As romantic and exciting as these legends sound, one must often wonder about their origins. However in 1853, when the lake level was lowered by 12ft, an ancient oak dugout canoe measuring 10ft by

2ft was found in the silt on the lake bottom.

The grassy path now descends to join the Hafod y Llan Quarry tramway. This quarry saw considerable development in the 1870's with the anticipation of a railway link from Beddgelert, up Nantgwynant to Betws-y-coed. Unfortunately, this was never to come to fruition. The only method of transportation to Porthmadog for shipment was from the bottom of a series of spectacular inclines terminating at Pont Bethania and from there to the Croesor Junction by horse drawn sledges. The quarry was short lived and closed in the 1880's due to the prohibitive transport costs.

The broad path that can be seen winding its torturous way up the hillside is part of the route to the summit of Snowdon using the "Watkin Path". Sir Edward Watkin was a wealthy railway magnate, who in the late 19th century constructed a chalet in the woods close to Pont Bethania. This chalet was built for the convenience of his friends who wished to climb Snowdon. Another of his entrepreneurial efforts was to attempt to construct a channel tunnel under the English Channel. A section of tunnel approximately 1 mile long was constructed at either side of the Channel before the project was stopped by the Government of the day. However, what he will always be remembered for is his "Path". The "Watkin Path" was presented to the nation in 1892. Sir Edward managed to persuade the Prime Minister of the time W.E. Gladstone, who was by then 84 years of age and in his fourth term of office, to officially open the "Watkin Path". On the 13th of September, Gladstone, who incidentally was holidaying at Penmaenmawr at the time, took up this duty. It was estimated that in excess of two thousand people braved the adverse weather. Gladstone and his wife travelled by open top carriage to a suitable rostrum, the location now commemorated with a brass plaque. With Lloyd George in attendance, Celtic hymns were sung and a number of political speeches were delivered to the assembled masses. Sadly not a word was said about the "Watkin Path". To make amends for this Sir Edward and Lady Watkin, with the Gladstones and a few friends walked the path the following day, many of the group reaching Bwlch y Saethau but only Lady Watkin and a friend reached the summit.

At the top of the falls can be seen the remains of a mill. This mill once housed waterwheels for the Hafod y Llan copper and lead mines. These waterwheels operated dressing floor machinery and roller crushers. Two mines working in conjunction in this area were the Hafod y Llan and Braich yr Oen. The latter was located above the falls on Yr Aran's spur. Close by in Cwm Merch, can be seen the remains of the Lliwedd mines. Unfortunately, as with the slate industry in the area, they all suffered as a result of the high cost of carriage. The operations were also affected by drought and frost, which interrupted the crushing and dressing operations. Records of these operations are very sketchy but it appears that mining commenced in 1762. In 1847 they recorded a yield of 150 tons of copper and 30 tons of lead. Operations at these mines continued until 1907 (a newspaper with this date was discovered underground in the Lliwedd mine).

The Walk: Exit the car park and walk along the track passing toilets on L and platform on R (from train exit platform R). Continue along track until a gate on R is reached (signed Ffridd Isaf) with footpath sign. Go R through gate and over railway track. Go along track to fork, here ½ R through swing gate and up track passing quarry hole on R. **1.** After crossing a number of stiles the track levels out and passes a kissing gate on L with sign "Footpath to Snowdon." Continue along the now grassy track, again crossing a number of stiles. Ascend into the quarry complex. **2.** At fork in track (close to quarry hole) take the L higher track, which climbs between the slate tips to reach a plateau. At the plateau follow fence on R (do not cross). Ascend the incline to end of the quarry workings. Cross the boggy ground on a series of slab steps and continue up to the wall on the ridge crest.

*** *Those Walkers wishing to take in Yr Aran can take a R at this point and climb up to the summit (see instructions at end of text).* ***

3. Descend the scree path to a wall gap and continue along grassy path to cross a stream. At next stream, cross this and then down L to a tramway (re-crossing stream on descent).

*** Walkers can at this point, cross the quarry complex then take a descending path R to join the Watkin Path and view the Gladstone Rock***

4. Go R following the tramway until it passes through a cutting followed by a raised embankment. L down an obvious path to join main path (Watkin Path). R along path passing water falls on L.
5. Immediately after passing through gate, just above farm, go R through gate and along woodland footpath. This path completes the final descent to the main road (A498) at Pont Bethania. **6.** At main road R (towards Beddgelert) for a short distance. Cross road and L along minor road crossing bridge over Afon Glaslyn. At left hand bend in road, with gate/cattle grid on right, (sign "Llyndy Isaf") go R following farm track. Pass in front of farmhouse and through yard. **7.** Cross over stile. Continue along and over next stile into open marshy area. Following fence on L until a stile is reached. Cross this fence and go into the woodland. Here the path forks, take the R fork with the path now passing close to the lakeside. **8.** Close to a footbridge go through the kissing gate and continue following the river. **9.** At lane to Sygun Mine go L and pass through gateway with No Entry road sign. Carry on up to mine entrance access gate. Here go R (footpath sign) and along track which soon

becomes a lane. Continue along this to a road bridge (R/H bend) **10.** Close to the bridge by "weight restriction" sign cross over wall stile and through an area of rhododendrons until a lane is reached. Cross this, keeping river on R. Over footbridge and along to main road. At main road L and continue along until the Royal Goat Hotel is reached. R to railway station and car park.

To visit Yr Aran, allow approximately 45 minutes extra.

At Bwlch Cwm Llan, **point 3**, go R following wall down to small col. L through wall gap then R, ignoring stiles on R. Path climbs following a wall to a small hollow. **A.** Follow wall around wet area and cross over stile. The path continues to climb passing R through a wall gap and ascends with wall on L to a stile on the ridgeline. **B.** R up to the summit following line of old fence posts. Return to **B** and cross over stile. The path now descends the ridge, keeping wall on R. A small cairn is seen just before the wall turns sharply R. **C.** At cairn descend grassy gully until the gradient eases here go R heading towards spoil heap. At spoil heap L down edge of heap to tramway. **D.** At R/H bend in tramway, continue down gully, following stream, to main tramway. Cross this and descend to Watkin Path. Go R joining route.

Refreshments:- "Caffi Gwynant", a converted chapel is at the bottom of the Watkin path and worth a visit. Although not at the end of the walk this is the only opportunity to visit this particular café.

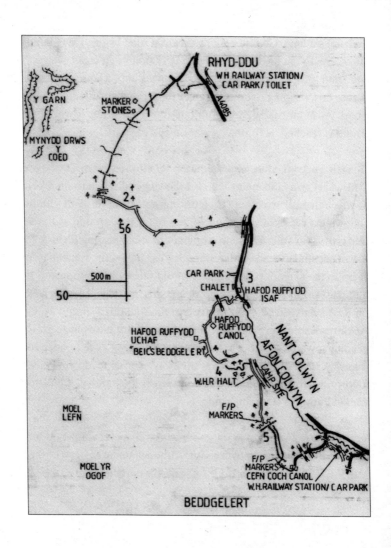

2. The Nant Colwyn Valley
From Rhyd-ddu to Beddgelert

Maps: 1:50,000 OS Landranger sheet 115 Snowdon/Yr Wyddfa (Caernarfon) or 1:25,000 OS Explorer sheet OL17 Snowdon/Yr Wyddfa.

Distance: 5 miles/8 kilometres.

Height gained: 375ft/109 meters.

Descent: 859ft/262 meters

Duration: 3 hours.

Terrain: Good forestry roads, can be wet at start and close to finish.

Stations/Halt: Rhyd-ddu and Beddgelert (Also a request halt close to the Forestry Camp site).

Car Park: Pay and display car parks in Beddgelert grid reference SH588481 and Rhyd-ddu grid reference SH571525 (close to halts/stations).

This walk can be accomplished when the weather does not allow you to venture onto the higher tops. It can also be used by mountain bikers, but a little care is required at the start and finish of the route. The walk starts from the station car park at Rhyd-ddu. This station was once the terminus of the North Wales Narrow Gauge Railway's extension to the Moel Tryfan undertaking. This extension line from the main route serviced both the Glanrafon and Ffridd quarries.

In spite of the stations locality, situated on an extremely exposed position at an altitude of 626ft (191 meters) and close to the lines summit at Pitts Head at 647ft (197 meters), the station's original buildings were considerably larger than other stations on the line.

The main buildings were constructed of brick and stone and there was a wooden refreshment hut for those passengers that were either waiting for the passenger service or a connection to Beddgelert by Charabanc. Nothing now remains of these buildings as the car park and toilet block are now located on the original site of the station.

The large house opposite the station was actually built as a hotel but unfortunately it was refused a license. Consequently, since then it has always been a private residence. The station has had a very chequered history. It was opened in May 1881 operating a passenger service, which continued up until part way through the hostilities of the First World War on 31st October 1916. The station was reopened on 31st July 1922, with the extension of the track down to Beddgelert opening on the 1st June 1923. This allowed a connection to a passenger service, which continued through to Porthmadog. Passenger services were again to cease on the 26th June 1937 due to the closure of quarries within the locality. This led to the final closure of the line even for freight on 19th June 1937.

The NWNGR must have thought there was a silver lining to all their efforts when, in spite of financial difficulties in 1875, C.E. Spooner Engineer to both the Ffestiniog Railway and the NWNGR proposed a rack railway be constructed to the summit of Snowdon. This would have led to an increase in the tourist trade in the Beddgelert area. Unfortunately for him, further financial problems caused the scheme to be dropped. It was fortunate for Llanberis because in 1893 a large deputation visited Assherton Smith, the local landowner and squire for Llanberis. He had been approached previously to ask if he would allow a railway to be built across his land to the summit of Snowdon. This time he agreed to the plan and as a consequence attracted tourism away from Beddgelert and into Llanberis.

The walk which roughly follows the course of Nant Colwyn continues into the Beddgelert forest and along the many forestry tracks. The current forest was first planted by the Forestry Commission in 1926. Forestry plantations were in existence prior to this date as information indicates that wood from the forest was utilised in the construction of the Porthmadog, Beddgelert and South Snowdon Railway. Again during World War 1 timber was transported, mostly horse drawn, from Cwm Ddu up to Rhyd-ddu and from Ty'n y Coed down to a point on the Beddgelert main road close to the Royal Goat Hotel.

The Walk: Depart the Station car park and cross the main road, to pass through a kissing gate. The path now crosses a boggy area on stepping slabs to a stream. Go L following stream to footbridge, now R over footbridge and across lane. Ascend bank following white paint marks to rejoin lane and up to road. Through lane gate and immediately L to pass through metal gate and along grassy path. Through gate and continue to stile, over this and up to a prominent boulder with a white painted arrow. **1.** At boulder go ½ L (boulder is junction with path to Y Garn) through gate and cross a stream. Continue on to cross a second stream. Pass through a gate into the forest, soon passing through a wall gap and crossing a forestry road. Pass between boulders and down to stream, now up onto bridge and L. **2.** Follow forestry road and at first junction go R and at next junction (T junction) go L towards main road. Cross railway track and immediately go R down forestry road to pass parking area and wooden chalet on R. **3.** At large property on L "Hafod Ruffydd Isaf" continue on for 50 meters then go R soon to cross a narrow road bridge over the river. Up to and over the railway track, soon passing "Hafod Ruffydd Canol". The road climbs to a T-junction, here go L. Pass lane to "Hafod Ruffydd

Uchaf" (Beic's Beddgelert). At fork continue on. At left hand bend (railway just in sight) go ½ R along footpath to join forestry road. Now go L down to railway track (near campsite). **4.** Just before railway track go R, forestry road runs parallel with railway track. Close to Campsite halt go ½ R up road passing barrier, continue on to sharp right hand bend. Here go L (footpath markers) to pass through a gate, cross a stream and through a second gate. **5.** The path now follows the wall on the R and passes through a field gate to cross to footpath markers (Moel Hebog path). Go L down path to buildings. Pass through a gate and down the track crossing the railway track. Continue on down passing a farm on the L.

At the railway bridge (over the track), go R and soon L passing under the railway line and up to the Beddgelert station (or L down to car park).

Refreshments: In Rhyd-ddu just down from the car park/station is the Tŷ Mawr tea room, open all year and supplying home baked produce this is a welcome halt anytime of the year. Further down the road is the Cwellyn Arms, which serves pub grub.

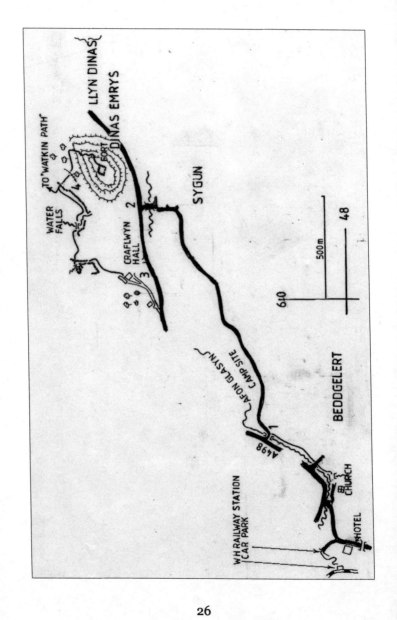

26

3. Visiting Vortigern's Fortress Dinas Emrys

Maps: 1:50,000 OS Landranger sheet 115 Snowdon/Yr Wyddfa (Caernarfon) or 1:25,000 OS Explorer sheet OL17 Snowdon/Yr Wyddfa.

Distance: 5 Miles/ 8 Kilometres.

Height gained: 872ft/ 266 metres.

Duration: 3 hours allowing time to explore.

Terrain: Good riverside paths, then short section on main road (500 metres) before a rocky path to summit which can be slippery when wet.

Stations/Halt: Beddgelert.

Car Park: Beddgelert (behind Royal Goat Hotel) on A498 south of village centre grid reference SH588481. Car Park is pay and display.

The walk out from Beddgelert is a very pleasant low level walk ideal for family exploration and will allow you to delve into Celtic Mythology and Arthurian legends of Dragons and Sorcery. The walk starts along a pleasant riverside footpath, which later passes close to the Sygun Copper mine. Unfortunately this mine is no longer extracting copper and has been developed into a thriving tourist centre. At Sygun the adventurous visitor can get kitted up with a miners lamp and follow the underground labyrinths followed by those miners of long ago. By entering the Victoria Level the budding miner can listen to a recorded commentary on the history of the mine which operated from 1825 until about 1901.

Care must be exercised when following the busy main road but all becomes tranquil when the drive past the lodge to Craflwyn Hall is reached. The hall's name "Craflwyn" is thought to have been a corruption of "Criafolen" meaning mountain ash or place of the mountain ash. Of course, these trees are in abundance in the area. The estate dates back to 1200AD, to the time when Prince Llywelyn the Great (Llywelyn ap Iorwerth of Gelert fame) donated land to the Cistercian Monks. The monks farmed this land as part of a Monastic Grange. Following Henry VIII's dissolution of the monasteries in 1536, the land was then farmed by Meredudd ab Ieuan, former steward of the monastic lands in the area. Probably following the marriage of the Steward's grand daughter Annes to Morys Jones, the estate passed into the ownership of the Jones family and by the early 1600's it was to become a gentry estate. The estate passed through the family from generation to generation carrying on the farming tradition. By 1873 it was to be run by Llywelyn Parry, whose initials and date appear on the gable of the lodge. He rebuilt the farmhouse and created a miniature estate, establishing woodland gardens and plantations. The family connection was severed after a period of 300 years when in 1895 the estate was sold. Unfortunately the property fell into disrepair due to the neglect of a succession of owners until it was obtained by the National Trust in 1994. They embarked on an extensive restoration programme. The Hall, restored to its former glory can now be used for conferences and weddings.

The walk passes over the slab bridge close to the falls of Afon y Cwm and then climbs into the mixed woodland surrounding Dinas Emrys and up to the fortress on the summit. Give yourself plenty of time to explore the remains of the 5th century hilltop fort and reflect on the mythology surrounding it. The story is left to us by the 9th century writer Nennius who tells us about the 5th century

Brythonic king Vortigern who invited the Saxons into his kingdom to help defend it. Unfortunately for him the Saxons were to try and oust him from his Kingdom and with the advice of his wizards he fled to Gwynedd to establish his sanctuary. During the construction of his fortress his daily inspection revealed that the work the masons had completed the previous day had been completely destroyed. In desperate consultation with his wizards he was instructed that in order to break the spell the masons should slake the mortar with the blood of an illegitimate child. A search throughout Britain eventually found a child and he brought this child to the site in preparation for his sacrifice. On hearing of the reason for his pending sacrifice the child instructed Vortigern to enter a cave located in the base Dinas Emrys. Here, Vortigern was to discover the reason for the continual collapse of the walls. Two dragons, one white depicting the Saxons and the other red depicting the Celtic nations were fast asleep. However on rising from their slumbers, they commenced fighting, which caused the fortress walls to collapse. The child was in fact Myrddin Emrys (Ambrosius) also known as Merlin. His prophecy saw the red dragon of the Celts being successful in battle with the Saxons. Vortigern was to finally find sanctuary on the Llŷn Peninsula in Nant Gwrtheyrn where he was to spend the remainder of his life in isolation.

Unfortunately we must now retrace our steps unless the walker wishes to continue to the "Watkin Path" and then around Llyn Dinas. This will lengthen the walk considerably.

The Walk: Unfortunately areas of the National Trust estate at Craflwyn do not allow dogs to pass through.

Depart from Beddgelert station and walk down to the car park. In the car park go R to main road (A498). Go L along road to bridge.

Cross the road and along lane, sign posted Gelert's Grave and Toilets, with river on L and cross footbridge. Go L still with river on L crossing lane and through gate. **1.** Continue along riverside path to a stile and lane. Cross stile and go R along lane to entrance of Sygun Mine. Here go L along access road to mine, crossing over bridge to main road. **2.** Go L along main road for 500m to National Trust sign for Craflwyn (do not take drive up to Hall at first NT sign). Go R up the drive passing lodge on L to car park. Here it is worth crossing the car park to read the information boards, which explain about other walks available at Craflwyn. Return to drive then go L towards Hall. **3.** At fork take L branch signed Stables/ Estate Office and pass between the rear of the hall and the converted stables and out through a gate into fields. Keep on along track to pass large enclosure on L. At end of track go L up to gate and continue on path passing through old wall gap. Here go R onto bridge and over stile (sign "Tir Gofal" Land being cared for). Keep going to nearby falls and cross slab bridge. Continue to wall corner and along with wall on R to stile. **4.** Go R over stile and then L up grassy bank passing through mixed woodland to fence with stile. Cross fence and up to summit and fortress. Explore.

To return to Beddgelert retrace your outward steps

For those wishing to make a longer excursion, after visiting the summit return to the wall stile and continue directly up the bank to a track. Here go R to eventually pass through old mine workings following marker posts to the "Watkin Path". To return to Beddgelert from this location descend to main road and pick up paths passing to the south of Llyn Dinas. Instructions for this return can be found in the Rhyd-ddu to Beddgelert, via Cwm Llan walk from 6. onwards.

Refreshments: Beddgelert has a number of cafes and pubs supplying a range of food. The Antique shop and Bistro close to the bridge is an old favourite. However with such a choice it is worth investigating any of the other places.

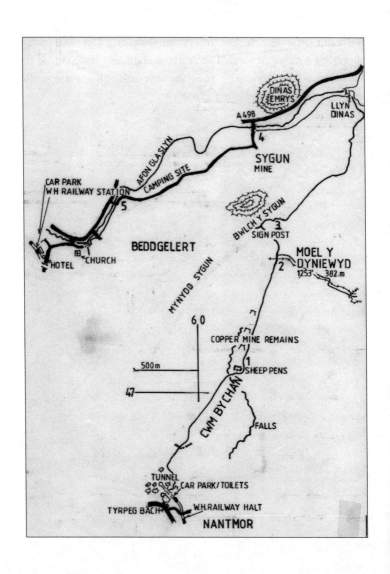

4. A walk up the Copper Mines Valley Nantmor to Beddgelert

Maps: 1:50,000 OS Landranger sheet 115 Snowdon/Yr Wyddfa (Caernarfon) or 1:25,000 OS Explorer sheet OL17 Snowdon/Yr Wyddfa.

Distance: 5 miles/8 kilometres (add a further 1½ miles/2.4 kilometres to visit and return from Moel Dyniewydd).

Height gained: 597 ft/ 182 metres.

Duration: 3 Hours. (Add 1hr if Moel Dyniewydd is visited).

Terrain: Good through out, mountain paths and riverside walks.

Stations/Halt: Nantmor and Beddgelert.

Car Park: Close to Beddgelert station (behind Royal Goat Hotel) on A4988 South of village centre grid reference SH588481 and also Aberglaslyn grid reference SH597461. Both car parks are pay and display.

This walk departs from the request halt at Nantmor, descending to the main road then climbing through the car park following signs for Cwm Bychan. Climb up the grassy valley passing close to the remains of the copper mining industry that once operated in Cwm Bychan. Sadly little remains of the industry that shaped this valley apart from spoil heaps and adits, most now overgrown. The rusting remains of the towers and turntables of the aerial tramway which used to transport the rough ore down the valley and away to be smelted are still visible. The strange cage by the railway bridge is all that remains of the tower, which was used to tension the tramway rope.

The first recorded mining operation was in 1720 and this continued in a very small way until its final closure in 1875. Unfortunately, in spite of the mines rather grandiose name "Cwm Bychan Silver and Lead Mine Co" the venture was a failure with almost no ore being extracted.

From the ridge the path climbs over Cwm Sygun where the remains on the upper workings on the Sygun Copper mines (Llwyndu level) can be seen. From here the path descends through an area that was once cleared of Rhododendrons. Down to Llyn Dinas from where the path follows Afon Gwynant to pass one of the most historic areas in Wales, the rocky outcrop of Dinas Emrys where a legend and fortress to Vortigern (Gwrtheyrn) is located. This subject is dealt with in the chapter on Vortigern's fortress which visits the summit of Dinas Emrys.

Close to Dinas Emrys, the remains of the Sygun Copper Mines can be seen. The site is now a museum depicting the whole of the copper industry in Snowdonia. Here tourists can venture into the bowels of the earth via the Victoria Level and listen to the recorded commentary on the history of the mine. The mine operated from 1825 to about 1901. The mine was to achieve brief fame in 1958 as the site of the Chinese village in the film "Inn of the Sixth Happiness" staring Ingrid Bergman. The film was based on the Alan Burgess novel *The Small Woman* and related the story of Gladys Aylward. She was an outstanding missionary working in war torn China in the 1930's, where she led 100 refugee children over the mountains and to the Yellow River to safety from Japanese invasion. So imagine that for a short time this part of Snowdonia was portrayed as China and for some period after was a tourist destination for the film enthusiasts who wanted to see the locations used in the film.

The path now continues to follow the river and back into Beddgelert.

The Walk: The walk starts from the request halt at Nantmor (until the halt is finished it is possible to start from Beddgelert and use the Fisherman's path as a link). Leaving the halt go L down to the main road, here go R for a short distance passing "Tyrpeg Bach" cottage (large Ammonite by front door). Go R into Aberglaslyn car park and up to top LH corner. Just before toilet block go L through gate and then R (sign posted Cwm Bychan). Go under railway bridge and continue on over grassy area (noting remains of old aerial tramway) up steps and R at junction. Continue ascending into a distinct valley to cross a stream on stepping stones. **1.** Pass to the R of old sheep pens and soon follow further remains of the aerial tramway. Continue up to the saddle and cross the fence. **2.** *Diversion**** From this location it is possible to visit Moel Dyniewydd by turning R and following the fence to the summit. The return follows the same route. This will add a further 1hr to the walk****.* The path now bears L providing the walker with good views of Moel Siabod, the Moelwyns, and the Cwm Tregalan area of Snowdon. **3.** At a flat area with evidence of mine workings and signpost go R to Llyn Dinas. Head down to Llyn Dinas admiring the views on the way. When the lake comes into view the path steepens considerably. At lakeshore go L and through kissing gate and then along the riverside path. **4.** Go through gate and L up lane passing Sygun Mine car park on L. Just before the entrance to Sygun Mine go R along lane. **5.** At bridge cross over stile and continue along riverside path to next gate, through this and cross lane to pass between wall and houses and to foot bridge. Go R over foot bridge and along lane passing toilets and shops on L and up to main road. L along main road to pass Tourist information centre on R. Soon after this go R into car park and up to the top LH corner to the gate to the Beddgelert Station. Through this and up to the station.

For those wishing to make a circular route to return to Nantmor this can be done by using the "Fisherman's Path".

Refreshments: Beddgelert has a number of cafes and pubs supplying a range of food. The Antique shop and Bistro close to the bridge is an old favourite. However with such a choice it is worth investigating any of the other places.

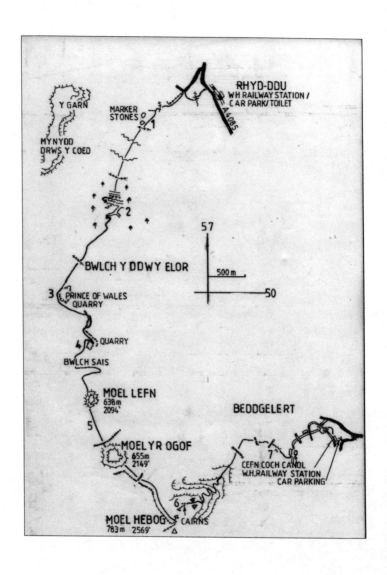

5. Over Moel yr Ogof and Elen's lofty ridges
Rhyd-ddu to Beddgelert

Maps: 1:50,000 OS Landranger sheet 115 Snowdon/Yr Wyddfa (Caernarfon) or 1:25,000 OS Explorer sheet OL17 Snowdon/Yr Wyddfa.

Distance: 7 miles / 11.26 kilometres.

Height gained: - 1,939 ft / 591 metres.

Duration: 6 hours.

Terrain: A true mountain mixture. Boggy at first then forestry tracks to steep grassy ascents, broad open ridges and gentle descending rocky scrambles.

Stations/Halt: Rhyd-ddu and Beddgelert.

Car Park: Pay and display car parks in Beddgelert grid reference SH588481 behind Royal Goat Hotel and close to Beddgelert Station. Also at Rhyd-ddu grid reference SH571525 close to station.

At the start this walk follows the same route as "The Nant Colwyn Valley, Rhyd-ddu to Beddgelert", and a detailed description of the station and the surrounding Industrial archaeology is included in that section. Do pause for a while to glance at the nearby Outdoor Centre, which was once the Rhyd-ddu School, home to one of the most outstanding literary figures in Wales. The poet, essayist and literary critic Syr T. H. Parry-Williams (1887-1975), came to prominence through the unprecedented feat of winning both crown and chair in the National Eisteddfod at Wrecsam in 1912 and again at Bangor in 1915.

The farm of Clogwyn y Gwin, situated to the north of the village, has a macabre connection with the supposed final shot to be fired at the battle of Waterloo. The tale revolves around the son of a farmer of Clogwyn y Gwin. Whilst the son was lying wounded, amongst the dead and the dying, awaiting medical attention for gunshot wounds to his kneecap, he noticed an old woman moving amongst the corpses. She was removing whatever valuables they possessed, dispatching with a mallet those who still had breath. Seeing the son raise himself she nodded as much to say "I'll deal with you later". Struggling, he lifted himself enough to raise his musket and taking careful aim shot her dead. That was reputed to have been the very last shot fired during the battle of Waterloo.

Leaving the forestry roads the path climbs steeply through the forest passing the remains of the Bwlch y Ddwy elor quarry, a small un-mechanised working operating in about 1883. The material extracted from here had to be transported by cart to Caernarfon. Later the path meanders through the remains of the workings of the Prince of Wales Quarry. During early operations the slates had to be transported by packhorse to Rhyd-ddu and then on to Caernarfon. In 1873 an extension was built to the Gorseddau Quarry tramway, which ran from nearby Cwmystradllyn to Porthmadog. This improved transport link allowed further operations to be carried out in the Prince of Wales quarry. Peak production was in the region of 5000 tons per annum with a workforce of some 200 men. The quarry closed in 1886. The path later climbs the flanks of Moel Lefn passing the remains of the small Princess Quarry and up to the broad ridge line.

The path passes over the summit of Moel yr Ogof ('bare round topped summit of the cave'). This area is thought to be the hiding place of the last Welsh Prince Owain Glyndŵr. In fact the cave in question is known as Ogof Elen, who was the wife of the Roman Emperor Macsen Wledig. It was also thought that Ieuan ap

Rhobert of nearby Gesail Gyfach also hid in this cave during the Wars of the Roses. Another small cave is in fact an old Asbestos mine. It's really thought that Glyndŵr's cave is located in the boulder field in Cwm Llwy under Moel Hebog.

The path now climbs to the summit of Moel Hebog where the walker can pause to enjoy some of the most spectacular views in Snowdonia. Ranging from Cader Idris to Snowdon and across to Aran Benllyn and Aran Fawddwy and the Arenigs before you finally head down into picturesque Beddgelert.

The Walk: Depart from the station/car park and cross the main road to pass through a kissing gate. The path now crosses a boggy area on stepping slabs to a stream. Go L following the stream to footbridge; here go R over footbridge and across lane. Ascend a bank following white paint marks to rejoin the lane and up to the road. Through lane gate and immediately go L to pass through metal gate and along grassy path. Through gate and continue on to stile. Over this and up to prominent boulder with white painted arrow. **1.** At boulder go ½ L (boulder is on junction with path to Y Garn) through gate and cross a stream. Continue on to cross a second stream. Pass through a gate into the forest, soon passing through a wall gap and crossing a forestry road. Pass between boulders and down to a stream. Go up L onto bridge and immediately R (sign Cwm Ddu). **2.** Up forestry road to T-junction, go R for 50 metres then L up rough path in forest. Path emerges from forest into open moorland and soon passes through gate (Bwlch yr Ddwy Elor, – 'pass of the two biers'). **3.** L to follow path descending into Quarries. Just after first quarry hole and remains of horizontal tramway keep to the mini valley bottom and pass close to open quarry hole. Rocky paths now becoming obvious skirting L to outcrops into cwm. Path crosses edge of marshy area to a wall.

Go R following wall (on occasions it is dryer on forest side of wall) and at earliest opportunity pass through wall to ascend steep gulley, with fence on L, to small quarry. **4.** Pass quarry hole by skirting R then continue climbing to cross the small marshy area of Bwlch Sais (pass of the English). Up through the rocky outcrop to climb the grassy ramp to the rock capped summit of Moel Lefn. **5.** The path now follows the broad ridge to pass just R of the summit Moel yr Ogof (interesting scrambling can be enjoyed by keeping to the rocks direct to the summit). The path now descends through a rocky area to a wet col and runs along side a wall with stepping-stones in places. Now down through a notch in the cliff to gain the lowest point on the ridge. Continue on now uphill keeping wall on R to the summit of Moel Hebog. From the summit of Moel Hebog follow a line of cairns along ridge (heading in the direction of Snowdon). **6.** Drop down through rocky area towards two large cairns on the ridge line. The path passes between these two cairns and then immediately R2 through rocky outcrops before descending to a grassy spur and on to the mountain wall. Pass through a gate and continue descending spur, now following way-marking posts. **7.** Cross a wooden bridge and head towards a barn. Through gate and go L down lane (Cefn Coch Canol) to cross railway track. Continue through farmyard and down to railway bridge. Immediately before bridge go R through gate and under railway line. At path junction go R up to station or L down to car park.

Refreshments: In Rhyd-ddu just down from the car park/station is the Tŷ Mawr tea room, open all year and supplying home baked produce. Further down the road is the Cwellyn Arms which serves pub grub.

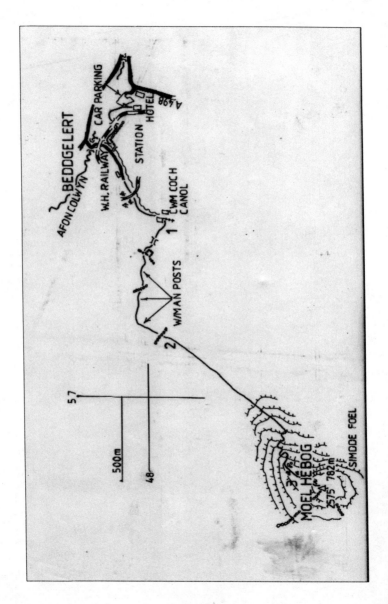

BEDDGELERT

AFON COLWYN

W.H. RAILWAY

CAR PARKING

STATION

HOTEL

A498

CWM COCH CANOL

1

W/MAN POSTS

2

500m

57

48

MOEL HEBOG

2575   782m

SIMDDE FOEL

6. Moel Hebog and the Hawk's Lofty Lair

Maps: 1:50,000 OS Landranger sheet 115 Snowdon/Yr Wyddfa (Caernarfon) or 1:25,000 OS Explorer sheet OL17 Snowdon/Yr Wyddfa.

Distance: 4 Miles/ 6.4 Kilometres.

Height gained: 2,431ft/741meters.

Duration: 4 hours.

Terrain: : Grassy ascent until craggy area is reached then scree path with very easy scramble sections, descent same way.

Stations/Halt: Beddgelert.

Car Park: Close to Beddgelert station (behind Royal Goat Hotel) on A4988 south of village centre grid reference SH588481. Car Park is pay and display.

Underneath Moel Hebog's lofty summit stands Beddgelert station; this little station has really not had a happy history. It wasn't until 1st June 1923 that a through service was introduced from Rhyd-ddu to Porthmadog and the possibility of rail travel from Beddgelert became a reality. Moel Hebog translates as the round flat-topped mountain of the Hawk.

Due to the success of a steam operated system on the Ffestiniog railway, encouragement was given for further undertakings in the locality. One such potential undertaking was a proposal in August 1872 for a junction at Betws-y-coed. From here a line was to run via Capel Curig descending Bwlch y Gwyddel and along the shores of Llyn Gwynant and nearby Llyn Dinas. It was to carry on to Beddgelert then join forces with the Croesor and Porthmadog

Railway to form a junction with the Croesor Tramway. This tramway then ran into Porthmadog. This ambitious link across Snowdonia never came to fruition. Another potential project was to construct a standard gauge railway from Porthmadog to a terminus at nearby Llyn Dinas. This again never materialised. It wasn't until 1903 when the Porthmadog, Beddgelert and South Snowdonia Railway company was amalgamated with the North Wales Electric Traction Company that things started to move foreword.

The North Wales Electric Traction Company's intention was to construct an electrified line in the area using power from nearby Hydro Electric schemes. A power station was constructed at Cwm Dyli in 1905 and is still in operation to the present day. The power station was to be used not only for the electrification of the railway but also to provide power for the nearby quarries and mines. It also provided power for Marconi's transmitting station at Cefn Ddu above Waunfawr. Little did the designers and contractors realise that the power station would outlive all of its original intended customers.

This little power station has played its part in the history of the area. Recently it celebrated over 100 years of almost continuous production of electricity except when the pipe from Llyn Llydaw was renewed and changed from twp pipes to one and modifications were made to the turbines in 1990. On a more bizarre note it was to feature as an extra in the James Bond movie "The World is Not Enough" starring Pierce Brosnan as Bond and Dame Judi Dench as "M". On that occasion it played the part of an oil pipeline and pumping station.

Returning to the history of the station, more problems were to beset it. In 1909 work on the line to Porthmadog was stopped although they did leave us with evidence of their attempts in the form of Afon Glaslyn tunnels and the bridge abutments close to the Royal Goat Hotel. It wasn't until 1922 that Beddgelert station was rescued when Sir Douglas Fox and Partners were contracted to survey the whole undertaking, with an upgrade of the line to Rhyd-ddu and to survey a new line to Porthmadog. Following the survey it was agreed to carry out the construction work, which was completed on the 12th May 1923 by Sir Robert Mc Alpine.

Departing from the station the walk climbs steadily through a number of farms crossing the loop of the railway and out into open moorland to continue climbing steeply up the flanks of Moel Hebog. As the easy scramble across the scree-covered flanks is negotiated another of Owain Glyndŵr's supposed hiding places comes into view, a cutting in the steep flanks of Moel yr Ogof (the bare round topped hill of the cave), which is in fact Ogof Elen (the cave of Princess Elen).

Close to Ogof Elen is a cave, which is often mistaken for the actual refuge. It is in fact the remains of an old Asbestos mine and the remains of the asbestos seam can still be located on the right hand wall. Now, finally at the summit the walker can keep a sharp watch for the hawks and birds of prey which frequent the area. Enjoy the panorama from the summit, which makes this ascent all the more worthwhile. To the west is Cwm Pennant and on out towards the Rivals and the Llŷn Peninsula. To the north are the Nantlle Ridge and the Snowdon ridges. Looking east, there is a view towards Cnicht and the Moelwyns and finally south towards Porthmadog and the coast.

The return of this walk requires a little care reversing the scree slopes but once on the grassy slopes the scenery of the beautiful Colwyn and Gwynant valleys and Beddgelert village far below can be appreciated.

The Walk: The walk can either be started from the car park by going through the wooden gate at the top corner and up to the station platform or from the station platform by following the easy angled path (descending) heading away from the village. At a sharp RH bend continue on to pass through a gate and under the railway line. Directly opposite a water tower pass through gate on L then R to follow the river. Pass through field gate and on to track, here go ½ L passing farm. The track ascends through a small area of pines and crosses the railway line. **1.** At Cwm Cloch Canol Cottage go R around side of barn and through gate. Continue along path. On reaching path junction go ½ L along paved path to cross a wooden bridge then cross to stile at corner of sheep pen. From stile follow ascending path following path markers then later cairns to pass through low wall and up to next wall with gate and stile. **2.** Through gate and continue ascending, passing cairns, towards the L edge of the craggy area. Soon the craggy area is reached and the path, taking a general ascending line, meanders through the outcrops to two large cairns on the subsidiary ridge. **3.** Continue ascending this ridge and through the next craggy area to the summit plateau and Trig point.

The Return: Follow the route of your ascent by initially walking along the promontory away from the "Trig" point, soon keeping steep ground on R. Descend through initial craggy outcrops to the two large cairns at position 3. Here pass between the cairns and immediately go R, descending the final rocky outcrop. Once the outcrops have been negotiated an easy descent brings the walker back into Beddgelert.

Refreshments: Beddgelert has a number of cafes and pubs supplying a range of food. On a hot day it would be difficult to resist ice cream from Glaslyn ices near the Pizza restaurant in the village centre. However with such a choice it is worth investigating any of the other places.

*Locomotive engine turning round its two coach trains at
South Snowdon in 1927. Llyn y Gadair in the background.*

*Train arriving at Snowdon Station in the mid 1890s. The name was changed
from Rhyd-ddu in 1893. Today the station is referred to as Rhyd-ddu.*

Southbound train on the biggest horseshoe curve just north of Beddgelert.

Train arriving at Beddgelert from Porthmadog in the summer of 1923.

S.W. Baker

'Russell' and train arriving at Beddgelert from Dinas in August, 1935.

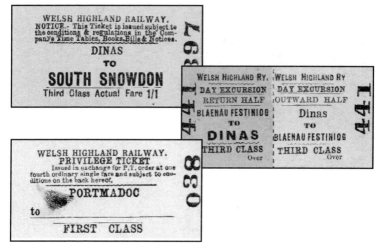

Card tickets typical of those used on the W.H.R. between 1923 and 1936.

S.W. Baker

Northbound train at the head of the Aberglaslyn Pass and about to cross Afon Glaslyn on Bryn-y-Felin bridge. July, 1936.

C.A. Appleton

Single coach train heading south in the Aberglaslyn Pass in 1927.

*Southbound train in the Aberglaslyn Pass exiting
one of the two shorter tunnels.*

H.F. Wheeller

The two short tunnels in the Aberglaslyn Pass; looking south. 1935.

Southbound train approaching Nanmor Station in 1923.

'Russell' and southbound train in harbour cutting. 1923.

Track of Croesor Tramway crossing the Nanmor to Llanfrothen road at Carreg Hylldrem after closure. 1947.

Ffestiniog locomotive 'Princess' with brake composite carriage at Croesor Junction. April 1926.

R.W. Kidner

Southbound train crossing Afon Glaslyn at Pont Croesor.
Cnicht in the background. 1934.

J.I.C. Boyd

Bridge over Afon Nanmor just south of Hafod-y-llyn in 1947.
An equivalent bridge is there today.

The head of the Croesor Tramway main line at
Blaen-y-cwm Power Station. 1968.

'Russell' and train approaching Porthmadog from the north.
Tremadog cliffs in the background. Mid-1930s.

Bont-y-cyt between Snowdon mill and the Cambrian Coast line.
1947 showing siding in to (flow) mill.

Train bound for the J.R.'s Harbour Station crossing
Porthmadog High Street.

C.L. Mowat

*Porthmadog New (1923) Station showing refreshment room
(at right angles to line of rail) and water tower.*

Studio Eryri

Snowdon flower mill.

59

S.H. Clifford

Train at Porthmadog New (1923) Station passing North Snowdon Mill seen above first carriage. 1934.

Slab bridge below Rhaeadr Cwm Llan

Remains of the Cwm Bychan Silver and Lead Mines' aerial tramway

Descending from Moel Lefn to Moel yr Ogof.

Looking up Cwm Bychan – 'Copper Mines Valley'

Descent from Moel yr Ogof

Afon Glaslyn in flood near Pont Croesor

Slab bridge over Afon y Cwm on the path to Dinas Emrys

Hafod at Llyn Lagi, looking towards Moel Hebog and the Nantlle ridge

Aberglaslyn gorge and the Fisherman's Path

Sculpture of a dog's paw on the gate leading to Gelert's Grave at Beddgelert

Clouds over Moel yr Ogof

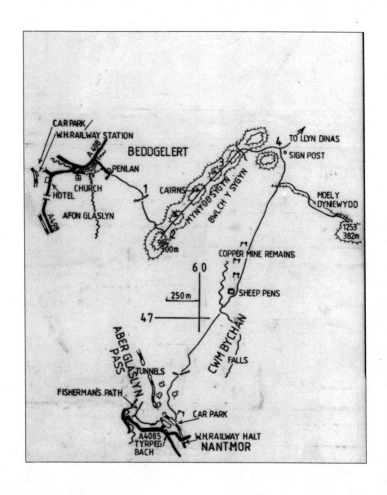

7. A walk with a Little Bear
Beddgelert to Nantmor over the ridges

Maps: 1:50,000 OS Landranger sheet 115 Snowdon/Yr Wyddfa (Caernarfon) or 1:25,000 OS Explorer sheet OL17 Snowdon/Yr Wyddfa.

Distance: 3 miles/ 4.8 kilometres (if taking in Moel Dyniewyd, out and back, allow a further 1½ miles/ 2.4 kilometres).

Height gained: 912ft/278 metres (1122ft/ 342 metres summit of Moel Dyniewyd).

Duration: 3 hours (Allow approximately 1 hr to visit and return from Moel Dyniewyd).

Terrain: Rocky ascent from village, later heathery hillside, good grassy path on ridge and valley. Some areas wet under foot.

Stations/Halt: Beddgelert and Nantmor.

Car Park: Pay and display car parks at Beddgelert grid reference SH588481 and Aberglaslyn grid reference SH597461.

This walk starts from picturesque Beddgelert and ascends quite steeply up "Mynydd Sygyn". On its way it passes the little white cottage "Penlan" where many fans, both young and old from the world over, come to pay homage to the author and illustrator Alfred Bestall. He is best known for the adventures of "Rupert the Bear and Chums".

Alfred Edmeades Bestall, born in Burma in December 1892, was the son of Methodist missionaries the Reverend Arthur Bestall and Rebecca Bestall. At the tender age of 12 due to his parent's overseas commitments, he was sent to boarding school at Colwyn

Bay. It was whilst at school that his talent was recognised and it led to him being accepted for an art scholarship at the Birmingham School of Art. Unfortunately due to the hostilities of the First World War he never completed his studies and was sent over to France as a Driver Mechanic. To keep himself occupied in his spare time he would sketch portraits of families of service men from photographs. Returning home in 1919 he took up an assignment to illustrate publications by both Enid Blyton and A.A. Milne, also illustrating for "The Tatler", "Punch" and "Bystander".

Bestall's love with Wales started at the age of 20 when he joined his parents in the village of Trefriw in the Conwy valley. Here he enjoyed walking and sketching the local area and after the war he returned to holiday in nearby Nantgwynant. In 1956 he decided to purchase a cottage in Beddgelert, which he named "Penlan" after the cottage in Trefriw where he had enjoyed many childhood holidays. To escape the pressures of work he decided to move there permanently in 1980.

By now Bestall was illustrating Endpapers, one such Endpaper depicted a group of frogs enjoying a singsong close to a waterfall, which inspired Paul McCartney's video for "Rupert and the Frog Song". At the age of 93 he was awarded the MBE but unfortunately due to his deteriorating health he was unable to travel to London to receive it. Sadly, he passed away shortly afterwards.

His passing was not only mourned by family and friends but by Rupert fans the world over. Those of us who are Rupert fans can picture Beddgelert as "Nutwood" and you don't have to scan many of his annuals to find Nantgwynant and Llyn Dinas in the illustrations. After ascending the Rhododendron clad hillside the path arrives at the broad ridge affording breathtaking views into Beddgelert and the surrounding mountains of Snowdonia. The path follows the ridge to the upper workings of the Sygun copper mines.

If time allows you may venture out to the remote summit of Moel Dyniewyd (Hill of the Young Bullocks).

Later the path passes under the track of the Welsh Highland Railway and into the Aberglaslyn car park. From here it is a short walk along the road to the Nantmor Halt. If the walker wishes the "Fisherman's Path" can be used to make a circular return to Beddgelert.

The Walk: Depart station car park and walk down to main road. Turn L and along main road to bridge, cross over road but not over bridge. Go along riverside lane (signposted Gelert's Grave and Toilets). Cross over footbridge and onto green in front of cottages. Head towards R/H end of row of cottages. At lane go L for 40 metres then R up a narrow lane, passing the cottage called "Penlan" on L. This was once the home of Alfred Bestall. At top of lane go through a gate and ascend steep rocky steps. **1.** At a flat area path swings R and eventually up to a kissing gate. After this gate the path still continues to the R through rhododendron bushes and heather to reach a view point overlooking the Glaslyn Estuary. **2.** At view point go L along ridge line following parallel with the valley below to reach a rocky knoll. Go ½ R to reach the base of a small rocky escarpment and join a grassy path. The path soon passes close to two tiny "Tarns" and up to a large cairn. **3.** Over crossing paths keeping to ridge crest to get the best views. At next cairn go R for 5 metres then go L scrambling up small rocky outcrop and then joining broad grassy path which heads into a rocky cwm. The path narrows and traverses the cwm up to a fence. Go L along fence and down to stile. Cross this and down through old workings to sign post. **4.** Go R along path signposted to Aberglaslyn. Continue along path and on to stile at fence, cross this and descend into valley passing remains of old workings. Soon you will pass by sheep pens

69

and cross the river on stepping stones. Through a wooden gate and descend to pass under the railway track and into the Aberglaslyn car park. Exit the car park to the main road. Here go L for 50 meters then L up to the Nantmor halt.

For those wishing to walk out to Moel Dyniewyd, at **4.** go R signposted Aberglaslyn and continue to stile over fence. Do not cross this, but instead continue on along path that meanders alongside fence. At stile (ladder) cross over fence and continue ascending with fence now on L (ignore next stile) to reach the summit. Enjoy the views before returning by the same route.

Those wishing to make a circular route to return to Beddgelert can follow the instructions for the Fisherman's Path from the Aberglaslyn car park.

Refreshments: Beddgelert has a number of cafes and pubs supplying a range of food. The Antique shop and Bistro close to the bridge is an old favourite. However with such a choice it is worth investigating any of the other places.

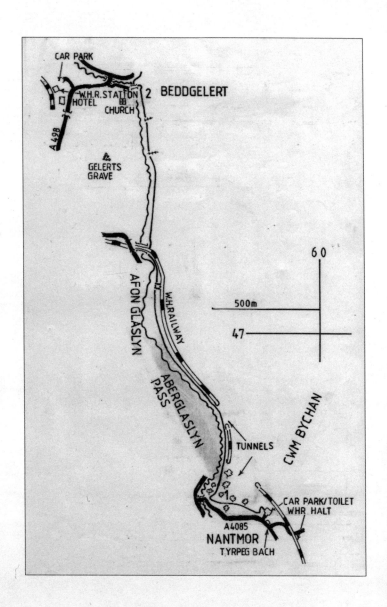

8. The Fisherman's Path
Nantmor to Beddgelert

Maps: 1:50,000 OS Landranger sheet 115 Snowdon/Yr Wyddfa (Caernarfon) or 1:25,000 OS Explorer sheet OL17 Snowdon/Yr Wyddfa.

Distance: 2 miles/3.3 kilometres.

Height gained: 75ft/ 22 metres.

Duration: 1½ hours.

Terrain: Good riverside path with assistance given in places.

Stations/Halt: Beddgelert and Nantmor.

Car Park: Pay and display car parks at Beddgelert grid reference SH588481 and Aberglaslyn grid reference SH597461.

This path, gentle at first, allows access to an area that was once the domain of anglers only. It is also an excellent vantage point to view the various species of birds whose habitat is the rocky river bed of the Aberglaslyn. The lower end of the path as it approaches the road bridge over Afon Glaslyn, has become known humorously as Wales' only "Via Ferrata" or "Iron Way" due to the hand holds that have been bolted in the rock to safeguard the walker. Have no fears, there is no need for any specialist equipment what so ever as the path is well constructed and quite passable for mere mortals.

The riverside path passes close to the church of St Mary, a very pretty and well maintained church which is well worth a visit. The church was built on the site of an Augustinian Priory, which Bishop Anian described in the 13th century as the most senior religious house in all Wales with the exception of Bardsey Island (Island of

Saints). The land on which the Priory was built was given to the Augustinian order as early as 1137 by Owain Gwynedd. Unfortunately in 1283 a fire swept through the building and all the chronicles and charters of the order were lost. The fire evidently did not destroy the Church although the roof may have been damaged. Bishop Anian begged Edward I to rebuild the Priory and although this was done, there is now no trace of his work as the last remains of the buildings were pulled down in 1830.

The obvious buttress in the field and the bridge over the road is the remains of the abortive attempt in 1906 by the Porthmadog, Beddgelert and South Snowdonia railway to construct a railway line from Beddgelert to the Croesor Junction. The North Wales Power and Electric Traction companies intended running a narrow gauge railway line from Beddgelert through the valleys to Capel Curig and on to Betws-y-coed. Unfortunately what can be seen is all that remains of this particular project as the scheme collapsed in 1909.

Pont Aberglaslyn, located at the bottom of the Glaslyn Gorge, is, according to legend another "Devils Bridge". It has been claimed the bridge was constructed by the Devil and for his efforts he made a bargain that he was to possess the soul of the first creature to cross over the construction. Robin Ddu, a local Magician was drinking in the "Tafarn Telyn" (Tavern of the Harp) and was called by the Devil to inspect his work. Robin Ddu agreed and assured the Devil his labours would not go unrewarded. On inspecting the bridge he told the Devil that he intended to throw a loaf of bread on to the bridge to see if it would hold its weight. All of a sudden a small dog darted after the loaf, thus fulfilling the bargain. With hoots of laughter Robin Ddu returned to his drinking companions, having fooled the Devil and fulfilled the pact.

Walk: Depart from the halt L down to the main road. Go R along main road for a short distance passing "Tyrpeg Bach" cottage (large ammonite by front door). Later go R into Aberglaslyn car park. Just before toilet block go L through gate and L into woods (sign post for Aberglaslyn). At path junction go L soon following fence on L. Descend to kissing gate at end of road bridge. Do not pass through this. **1.** Go R following path with river on L. Later cross over railway track and continue along to footbridge over river. **2.** Go L crossing over footbridge and along riverside path to lane. Along lane and up to main road. Here go ½ L along main road for 150 metres and then R into car park and Station. If the halt at Nantmor is not open at the time you choose to do the walk, then it will be necessary to return along the same route to the car park. This will double the time and distance taken for the walk but as it is one of the shorter excursions this should not prove to be a great hardship.

If you wish, you can follow the footpath that goes on the R/H side of the river to reach Beddgelert. Please note that the addition of this walk can be used to make a circular route for a number of walks listed in the book.

Refreshments: Beddgelert has a number of cafes and pubs supplying a range of food. The Antique shop and Bistro close to the bridge is an old favourite. However with such a choice it is worth investigating any of the other places.

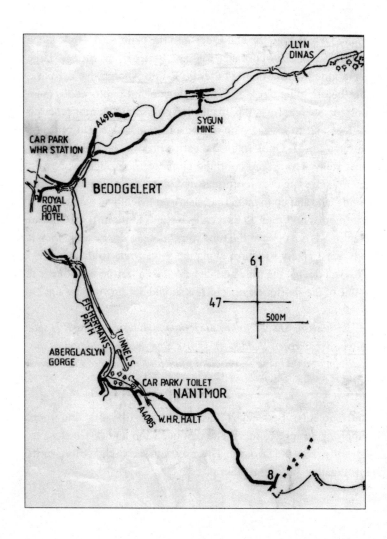

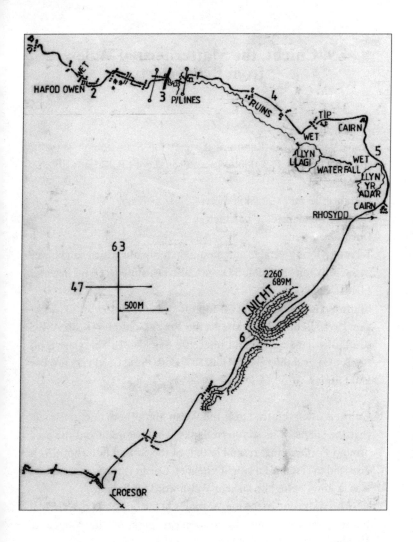

HAFOD OWEN 2

3 P/LINES

4

RUINS

TIP

CAIRN

WET

LLYN LLAGI

WET

WATERFALL

5

LLYN YR ADAR

CAIRN

RHOSYDD

63

47

500M

2260
689M

CNICHT

6

7

CROESOR

9. Cnicht, the Matterhorn of Wales from Beddgelert

Maps: 1:50,000 OS Landranger sheet 115 Snowdon/Yr Wyddfa (Caernarfon) or 1:25,000 OS Explorer sheet OL17 Snowdon/Yr Wyddfa.

Distance: 13 miles/20.9 kilometres.

Height gained: 2,126ft/ 648 metres.

Duration: 7 hours.

Terrain: Good riverside and mountain footpaths which can be wet in the proximity of "Hafod Owen", also wet close to Llyn Llagi and Llyn yr Adar.

Stations/Halt: Beddgelert / Nantmor.

Car Park: Beddgelert (close to the Royal Goat Hotel) on A 498 south of village centre grid reference SH588481. Aberglaslyn off the A4085 grid reference SH462597. Both these Car Parks are Pay and Display.

Cnicht is often referred to as the Welsh Matterhorn due to the fact that the shape of its southern flanks, when viewed from the area around Porthmadog, resemble that of the Swiss Matterhorn. It is also said to resemble a knight's helmet, Cnicht (the c is pronounced k as in king) being the ancient Welsh word for knight.

This walk, one of the longer routes in the book and of a circular nature, departs from the station/car park in the village of Beddgelert and follows Afon Gwynant up to Llyn Dinas. On your way you will pass the Sygun Copper mine and the ancient fortress of Dinas Emrys. Later the route crosses out of the Gwynant valley into the Nantmor valley and ascends to the shores of Llyn Llagi, the first of a number of high mountain lakes passed during the course of the walk.

On Llyn Llagi's north west shore the remains of an ancient settlement can be found. This was thought to be a "Crannog", which were dwellings supported on stilts situated either in the lake or on artificial islands, giving sanctuary from enemies or wild beasts. These dwellings were inhabited by the "Beaker People", a fair-haired race who had not yet developed the ability to work metal and had little contact with those who could. This consequently gave credence to the theory that these were the original "Tylwyth Teg" people, who were claimed to have a fear of metals. This may also have been re-inforced when tribes bearing metal weapons came over from the continent and conquered them. Later the "Tylwyth Teg" were to become known as "The Fair People", "Fairies" and even referred to in some areas as the "Little People."

Llyn Llagi was also a popular fishing location with James Spooner, the architect of the near by Ffestiniog Railway. From Llyn Llagi an ascent is made to Llyn yr Adar (Lake of the Birds), Llyn y Cwn (Lake of the Dogs) and Llyn Edno (also Lake of Birds) where the habitat and wet nature of the surrounding area has encouraged a diversity of wildlife.

Close by, Moelwyn Mawr comes into view overshadowing the remains of the Rhosydd and Croesor quarries. Both these quarries were classed as medium sized undertakings of their type and both suffered very mixed fortunes. The Croesor quarry, which was worked from 1850 was to close in 1878 but re-opened under the energetic management of Moses Kellow in 1895. During this latter period of the Welsh slate industry; the quarry produced some 5000 to 6000 tons of dressed slate per annum. Unfortunately the decline of the early 1900's and hostilities of the 1st World War saw the

Croesor quarry finally close in 1930.

Moses Kellow's ingenuity helped to make the quarry a technically advanced operation. He was instrumental in replacing water wheels with more efficient water turbines. He also turned his attention to the ventilation of the quarries and did much to improve air circulation. He was also responsible for developing the system of backfilling old worked out workings so that there was little visible evidence of the spoil heaps.

To the left, at the head of the Croesor valley can be seen the spectacular Rhosydd to Croesor incline, the highest pitch incline in the slate industry. To the right of the incline is the Fron Boeth tunnel, a tunnel of some 500m being the longest tunnel ever cut for horse drawn transport in the industry, unfortunately a roof fall prevents exploration of this tunnel.

Rhosydd quarry developed from small hilltop workings in 1830 to become a considerable undertaking with 15 levels and 170 chambers. The production of dressed slate in 1883 was 5616 tons with a work force of 192 men. It is mentioned in the history of Rhosydd that the quarry choir was so poor they could not afford the luxury of a tuning fork; a shackle was rung on a rail to give a perfect "C".

Unfortunately the demise of Rhosydd was due to the fact that the slate had to be transported on horseback crossing the boundaries of a number of neighbouring quarries. These quarries consequently imposed quite considerable taxes on the Rhosydd slate making it costly in comparison. In 1864 the finely engineered incline was opened allowing slate to be brought into Croesor and then on to Porthmadog. This incline was used until the quarries closure in 1930. It was in fact worked for a few years in the 1950's on a very small basis by a syndicate of local quarry men, but unfortunately the minimal returns forced the final closure of Rhosydd.

The path continues over Cnicht's lofty summit before descending steeply towards the Croesor valley. As is the case for most places with Celtic names, there is usually a number of theories as to how the village or area gained its name. Usually there is a romantic version of the derivation and a boring version to counteract it. Croesor is no exception to this rule. Legend would have us believe that the valley derives its name from a sad tale involving Princess Helen of Sarn Helen fame, who was married to the Roman Emperor Maximus. She was returning to the fort at Segontium (Caernarfon) with her protecting squadron of Legionnaires when she stopped in the remote valley to rest and drink from the spring, now known as Ffynon Helen (Helen's Spring grid reference SH629449). It was while she was resting she received news that her son, who was travelling south to meet her, had been attacked and killed by the Giant Cidwm (of Castell Cidwm fame at Llyn Cwellyn). On being told the news Helen broke down in despair and wept "Oh croes awr" (oh cursed hour) hence from that day, the valley and village became known as Croesor.

Sadly the more appropriate translation appears to mean boundary cross, "Croes". A cross-shaped post to mark a border or boundary in a mountainous area. However, why should we let the truth stand in the way of a good story.

The Walk: Depart station car park and walk down to main road. Turn L and along main road to bridge, cross over road. Go along riverside lane (signposted Gelert's Grave and Toilets). Cross over footbridge and L along riverside path crossing lane and continuing alongside river to stile. Cross the stile onto lane and continue along this, later to pass in front of the Sygun Copper Mine. **1.** Follow road around to bridge where the riverside footpath continues (½ R), follow this to the lake (Llyn Dinas). At lakeshore continue along footpath keeping lake on L until a stile is reached. Cross this and take ascending path ½ R. Cross stile by ruin and continue down with fence on R until a stile over this fence is reached. Cross this and enter wood. Path ascends through wood, passing ruin on L crossing stile over fence and on. Path meanders slightly but continue on towards cottage and pine trees taking care when negotiating boggy area close to the cottage. **2.** Over stile at gable end of cottage (Hafod Owen), R passing in front of cottage and through wall gap L. Path follows wall on L, towards pine trees. Cross stile close to pine trees and continue on with wall on R, crossing track to cottage until a stile over wall on R is reached. Cross stile and continue on with wall now on L climbing steep bank and through wall gap. Now follow mini ridge ½ L to cottage. **3.** Cross minor road and through field gate to follow track to cottage. Pass in front of cottage and down to stream, crossing stream and up to house. Cross stile and at far end of house R, under power lines and up towards wall. At wall, with gate and stile, continue up through craggy area, here the path crosses the stream and runs parallel with it. Just after ruin pass through wall gap, continue to next ruin and through wall gap. **4.** Path now heads towards waterfall on skyline; continue in this direction until a lake comes into view (Llyn Llagi). L up to spoil heap and ruin, here the path becomes more distinct continuing up to cairn on R. Path very indistinct at first but improves as it ascends to the top of a rise, where it dips and then ascends to a grassy col. Here Llyn yr Adar comes into view. **5.** Skirt to the L of the lake avoiding the wet areas and up to a large cairn on the ridge line, a meeting of a number of paths. R up hill following a rocky rib to Cnicht's summit. **6.** From the summit the path descends on the R of the ridge eventually changing over to the L to descend a rocky gulley to a large grassy area. Continue along ridge until path skirts to R of a craggy dome and crosses a stile over wall. The path now follows along the crest of the grassy ridge, vague in places, until it descends to a gate and stile, cross the stile and down to a track. L down to track junction. **7.** At track junction through gate and R following track heading towards pine trees in the distance. Continue along track until it descends to a minor road. **8.** Cross road and continue up minor road until it descends through village (Nantmor) crossing railway line (at some stage a halt will be built here and when that happens it will be possible to catch the train back to Beddgelert) and down to road. R along road and R into car park. Just before toilets, go L through gate and immediately L over stile and up to rise L. Pass through gate and into woodland. Path drops to a kissing gate (access to road bridge) do not go through this but turn R following river up the Aberglaslyn Gorge. This is the "Fisherman's Path", which takes you to a railway and footbridge crossing over the river. Do not cross over bridges but continue along concreted footpath to footbridge in village. L over bridge and up to road junction. L along road to the "Royal Goat Hotel" and go R into car park and Station.

Refreshments: Beddgelert has a number of cafes and pubs supplying a range of food. The Antique shop and Bistro close to the bridge is an old favourite. However with such a choice it is worth investigating any of the other places.

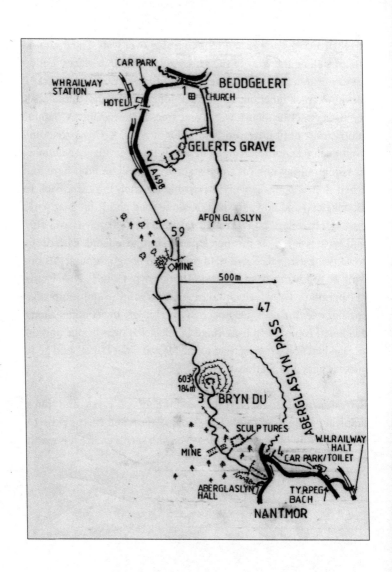

10. A walk with a Big Dog
Beddgelert to Nantmor

Maps: 1:50,000 OS Landranger sheet 115 Snowdon/Yr Wyddfa (Caernarfon) or 1:25,000 OS Explorer sheet OL17 Snowdon/Yr Wyddfa.

Distance: 2 .5 miles / 4 kilometres.

Height gained: - 459ft / 140 metres.

Duration: 1¾ hours.

Terrain: Good path through farmland and forest although the descent through the forest may be slippery under foot.

Stations/Halt: Beddgelert and Nantmor.

Car Park: Pay and display car parks at Beddgelert grid reference SH588481 and Aberglaslyn grid reference SH597461.

The walk departs from the station at Beddgelert and passes close to the "Royal Goat Hotel". In 1802 the "Royal Goat" was built by a Thomas Jones. It quickly became one of Snowdonia's great hotels, offering guiding services for the wealthy up to Snowdon's lofty summit. Its name was not in fact the "Royal Goat" but the "New Inn" and it wasn't until the hotel received a visit from the King of Saxony in 1844 that the name of the hotel was changed.

Many walkers will be familiar with the legend of the hound "Gelert", however for those who may not have heard the story the following is a brief resume. In the 12th Centaury Llywelyn ap Iorwerth, the Prince of Wales, whilst holding court in Beddgelert, would often take time to enjoy a days hunting in the nearby woods. On returning to their lodge after a successful days hunting, Llywelyn discovered his faithful hound "Gelert" covered in blood. Standing over his sons upturned cot and in a terrible rage, he feared the dog had murdered his son. Believing the worst he drew his sword and plunged it into the hounds great chest. As the hound lay dying, Llywelyn heard a cry from under the cot. With a pounding heart he lifted the cot to find his infant son completely unharmed. He then noticed that lying close to the cot was the body of a large wolf. In his anger Llywelyn had killed the dog that had fought and killed the large wolf thus saving his sons life. How bewildered the brave hound must have been to receive the sword instead of words of praise. With a heavy heart and deciding that "Gelert" shouldn't be forgotten, the faithful hound was laid to rest in a grave fit for a Nobleman, that grave still exists today for all to see.

Unfortunately this delightful, but sad story was a figment of the imagination of a number of villagers who in the late 1700's and early 1800's realised the need to encourage tourism to the area. David Pritchard, who was to become landlord of the "New Inn", along with a number of supporters for the project contrived to concoct the legend. The interest in the legend brought people from miles around to see the grave. The landlord and the villagers prospered from the increased numbers of tourists visiting and it could be said that the village is still benefiting today.

Ironically, in 1821 David Pritchard suddenly passed away at the age of 52, his death being so untimely that he had not even drawn up a will. Perhaps it was irony or a joke by Llywelyn's spirit that the instigator of one legend became one himself. Some weeks after his funeral, ghostly goings on were heard in the inn. All the villagers were held in the grip of fear. All that is, except his friend Huw. One evening whilst tending his cattle, Huw turned to find the ghostly apparition of his dear friend standing close by. With pounding pulse Huw was lead by the ghost to the inn where he was instructed to lift one of the great hearth stones. Under one of these he would find a purse containing a great deal of money and for returning this purse to David's wife he would receive the sum of two gold coins. He succeeded in locating the purse and he returned it to the innkeeper's wife and family. The ghostly figure has never since returned to the inn, but if you chance to indulge in the hospitality of the "Royal Goat Hotel" you may still hear David Pritchard's laugh when parting company with your money.

The walk passes the grave and memorial to the faithful hound and in the remains of a building can be seen the sculpture of a dog, presumably of Gelert, by the sculptor Rawleigh Clay.

The Walk: Depart from the station car park and walk down to main road. Turn L and along main road to bridge. Do not cross the bridge instead cross over the road. Go along riverside lane (signposted Gelert's Grave and Toilets). **1.** Just before footbridge go R through gate (signposted Gelert's Grave) and follow path with river on L. At path junction turn R (signposted Gelert's Grave). Pass gravesite and continue on to small enclosure/ruin. This ruin contains a statue of Gelert. Exit ruin and turn R through wooden gate and into field. Cross to track and continue up to main road. **2.** Cross main road and over railway track. After railway track continue along grassy track which is level at first. Pass through gate and into next field. Cross the field to a stile in the R.H corner. Over stile and continue ½ R between spoil heap and ruin. Path then gradually climbs up before finally reaching a viewpoint. **3.** Exit viewpoint and return to path, now turn L. Soon, go over stile and into the forest. Turn L, descending the path, which follows way marker posts. Keep a look out for the remains of a miner's cottage on the L, which contains some interesting sculptures. Descend to a stream with a bridge and pass through hole in fence. Turn L and follow fence to main road.

Now L along road to a bridge. Cross this and go through kissing gate at end of bridge. **4.** Turn R ascending steps with fence on R. Go through woods and descend into Aberglaslyn car park. Exit car park at main road and go along road. In a short distance turn L up a side road to Nantmor and the railway halt.

This walk can be made into a circular walk back to Beddgelert by joining the "Fisherman's Path" at point **4.** of this walk.

Refreshments: Beddgelert has a number of cafes and pubs supplying a range of food. On a hot day it would be difficult to resist ice cream from Glaslyn ices near the Pizza restaurant in the village centre. However with such a choice it is worth investigating any of the other places.

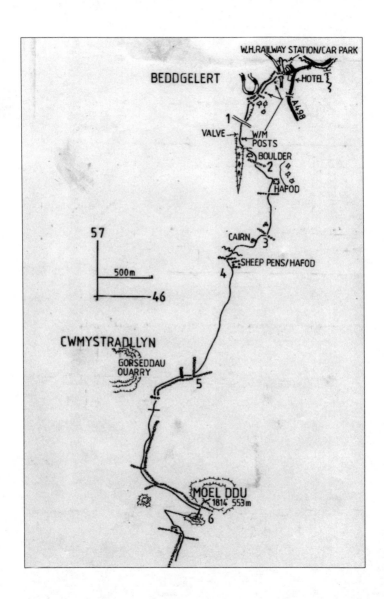

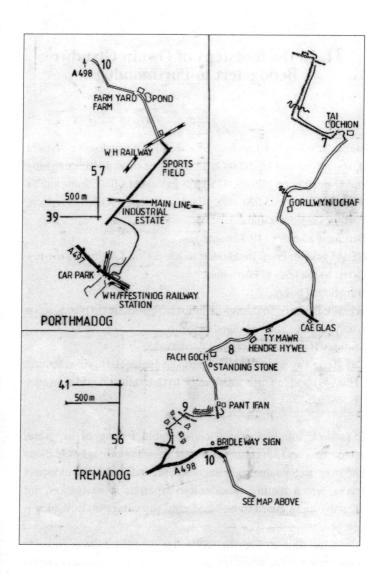

11. In the footsteps of Owain Glyndŵr
Beddgelert to Porthmadog

Maps: 1:50,000 OS Landranger sheet 115 Snowdon/Yr Wyddfa (Caernarfon) and 1:50,000 OS Landranger sheet 124 Porthmadog and Dolgellau or 1:25,000 OS Explorer sheet OL17 Snowdon/Yr Wyddfa and 1:25,000 OS Explorer sheet OL18 Harlech, Porthmadog and Y Bala.
Distance: 12 miles / 19.3 kilometres.
Height gained: From Beddgelert to Moel Ddu 1,679ft/ 512 metres. Down to sea level at Porthmadog.
Duration: 7 hours.
Terrain: Large open cwms with indistinct paths, wet in places, steep grassy hillsides and woodland descents.
Stations/Halt: Beddgelert and Porthmadog.
Car Park: Pay and display car parks at Beddgelert grid reference SH588481 and in Porthmadog close to the station at grid reference SH569385.

This walk will give you a considerable feeling of exposure, remoteness and adventure as it walk contours through wild cwms and over craggy summits. Sometimes, the walk is on very indistinct tracks, which require considerable expertise in navigation, not allowing one's guard to be lifted until the village of Tremadog is reached.

As the walk crosses the footbridge over the railway pause to glance down to see where the construction teams have had to widen the cutting to enable the larger locomotives to pass through. In the past some locomotives have had to have their elegant lines destroyed to enable them to pass through narrow cuttings and tunnels, which are a common feature of the Welsh Highland Railway.

This walk takes you along ancient paths above the tree line below the steep flanks of Moel Hebog (The bare flat topped mountain of the Hawk) into Cwm Llwy and Cwm Cyd. In this area above the rocky outcrops of Muriau Gleision, Owain Glyndŵr would come and train his troops. Close by are the ruins of the fort Pen y Gaer, which may have been used during these times for training and as a post to guard the back door into Eryri.

Around the year of 1409, Owain was being constantly harassed by the forces of Henry 5th. He would often spend time in the company of the poet Rhys Goch. His home was at Hafod Garegog, approximately 1 mile south of the current Glaslyn bridge on the east bank of the river Glaslyn. It was whilst being entertained by the poet that a guard in a nearby watchtower saw English soldiers approaching, obviously out to capture Owain. With out more ado Owain fled, swimming the Glaslyn estuary and then into the cwms below Moel Hebog. Whilst here, he noticed more soldiers approaching over Cwm Cyd. Frantic to avoid detection and capture, he scrambled up Moel Hebog's south east flank where he hid in Simdde'r Foel, thus escaping Henry's forces.

Legend has it that he was helped by Rhys Goch, other stories stated he hid in the craggy area called Diffwys on Moel Hebog's north east flank where he was helped by the Abbot of the Abbey at Beddgelert. However from this time on Owain vanished into obscurity, surfacing occasionally in the history books dealing with myths and legends. Perhaps, like King Arthur, he has been waiting until his countrymen were threatened and he could return again to lead them into battle.

As the ridge line of Cwm Oerddwr is reached, there are spectacular views of Llyn Cwmystradllyn and the Gorseddau quarries. Llyn Cwmystradllyn is now stocked for fishing and overseen by the Pwllheli Angling society. Their keen nurturing of stock gave a return of a 4lb Rainbow trout in the early 1990's. The dam was constructed in 1959 giving a maximum depth of 72ft, with further work carried out in 1976 and later in 1981.

The Gorseddau is classed as a most spectacularly unsuccessful undertaking. Quarrying in this area started in the early 19th Century and in 1855 the development increased to huge proportions. The operations were located on nine floors with extensive water courses being constructed from Llyn Cwmystradllyn to power the tools used at the nearby mill at Ynys y Pandy. All that remains of the mill, Tŷ Mawr, is now a stark windowless and roofless skeleton, towering above the road. The building was constructed by Robert Gill and John Harris between 1855 and 1857 to manufacture all kinds of slate products, not only roofing slates but cisterns, tanks, wine coolers, urinals, bread pickling containers, feeding troughs, monumental work, clock faces and sundials etc.

If the waste tips close to Tŷ Mawr are anything to go by, very little was produced, with the mill closing in 1877. According to local tradition Tŷ Mawr was utilised as a village hall, a chapel and in the 1880's an eisteddfod was held in the building. In the early 1900's the scrap man was to have his input and Tŷ Mawr was gutted leaving only what remains standing today. As part of the quarry workings a railway was constructed, in conjunction with nearby Cwm Pennant's Prince of Wales quarry, all the way into Porthmadog joining up with the line from Croesor Junction. Unfortunately in spite of all this development and investment the average annual output, with a work force of 200, was only 1400 tons, increasing to 2148 tons in the early 1860's. The quarry unfortunately was to close in 1867.

Later the walk descends into the village of Tremadog. This was the birth place of T.E.Lawrence (Lawrence of Arabia). Carry on into Porthmadog, passing over the remains of the railway from the Gorseddau and Moel y Gest quarries.

The Walk: Depart the station and walk towards houses (walkers starting in car park walk up to the station then L towards houses). Go through field gate and R up to and over foot bridge over railway track. Pass through kissing gate. Walking man posts will guide you across the field keeping wall on R. Over stile, or through gate and up wooded field with wall on R, later passing through wall gap. Go ½ L crossing field and up to gate. **1.** Cross track and through opposite gate to find a Walking Man post. Up field, passing old valve used for water supply, and up to a gate in the wall at top L of field. Through gate and ½ R ascending for 50 meters (passing to the L of a conspicuous boulder) and on to the remains of a wall. L along the wall to a wall gap. **2.** A small path, wet in places and indistinct at first, starts at this location gaining the base of a broad ridge approximately 100 meters above the tree line. Continue contouring the hillside and pass through another wall gap (remains of a Hafod below). Pass a cairn and carry on up to and through wall gap. **3.** At first keep close to wall on L and pass cairn. Path now descends gradually into valley and crosses a stream. Pass through old wall gap and on to sheep pen. Pass this on R and on to a low broken wall on L (passing ruined Hafod on L). **4.** At wall junction R uphill following a small stream and pass over a ruined wall. The path now aims for the intersection of the top wall with the ascending wall from the valley. Aim to this point to pick up a grassy path. Up and over a stile, continue ascending with wall on L up to ridge crest. **5.** The Gorseddau quarries and Llyn Cwmystradllyn now come into view. Cross wall and descend keeping as close as possible to wall on L. Pass through wall gap, now heading away from the quarries, and across a marshy area to a gate in the wall opposite. Through gate and climb steeply, keeping wall on L before eventually passing through gate in wall. Continue to col using the wall on L as a guideline. **6.** Stile to Moel Ddu is now on your L, slightly out of sight at first, cross this and up to summit. Return to stile and cross col to ascend subsidiary summit. Here go R following a broad ridge down to col then L down to wall. At wall L with wall on R passing a small enclosure and continue on to a small wall gap. Here R down hill with wall on R crossing a stream and down to wall corner. L following wall, still on R, to field gate. Do not go through this but cross ½ L to metal field gate close to buildings " Tai Cochion".

7. Through gate and down to grassy track, R along track. At junction close to house, go R continuing along track, which later improves, to "T" junction with road "Cae Glas" opposite. R up road passing over cattle grid and close to "Tŷ Mawr". At next cattle grid go L (sign posted "Hendre Hywel") and down track. **8.** At sharp L/H bend continue on up track to "Fach Goch" and through farmyard. Continue along track passing standing stone on L and down to buildings "Pant Ifan". Path passes between buildings and through a field gate. ½ R to run close to a wall, eventually passing R through a wall gap and running in front of craggy area. **9.** Path follows wall on L to pass through a gate and L steeply down in woodland crossing a stile and dropping down L steeply into field. Follow fence on L over stile and on to road. Follow this down to main road. L along main road for 400 meters to a bridle way sign with a sign for "Plas Tan yr Allt" attached to it. **10.** Cross road and along lane passing through farmyard and between buildings to pass a pond on L. Along track to pass over Narrow Gauge railway track and on to "T" junction. R along lane passing sports centre on L and over Main Line railway track. At end of industrial estate, L along footpath running on embankment to main road. Cross main road to station. To car park, pass station on L over bridge and first L.

Refreshments: There is a good choice of pubs and cafés in Porthmadog. Alternatively, in the summer months or weekends "Eric's Café" (Eric Jones the well known mountaineer and adventurer) on the Tremadog to Beddgelert road is well worth a visit even if its only to sit with the rock climbers who have spent the day on the near by crags.

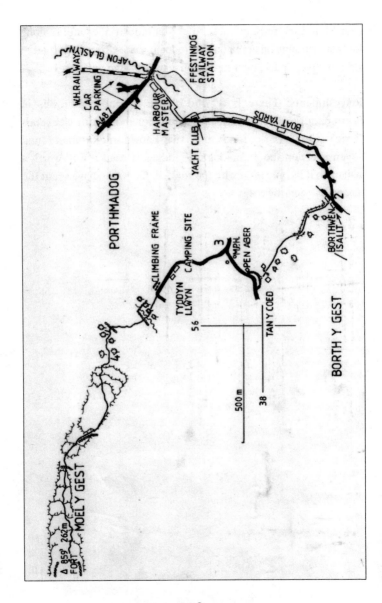

98

12. Moel y Gest to view Cardigan Bay

Maps: 1:50,000 OS Landranger sheet 115 Snowdon/Yr Wyddfa (Caernarfon) or 1:25,000 OS Explorer sheet OL17 Snowdon/Yr Wyddfa.
Distance: 4½ miles/ 7.24 kilometres.
Height gained: 859ft/ 262 meters.
Duration: 3 hours.
Terrain: Easy going on lanes, then considerable amounts of mixed woodland. On summit ridge of Moel y Gest there is some very easy scrambling.
Stations/Halt: Porthmadog Terminus.
Car Park: At Porthmadog Terminus and close by the harbour at grid reference SH569385 (pay and display).

This walk leaves from the terminus of the Welsh Highland Railway and crosses over to the Ffestiniog Railway Terminus. Here you can view the handsome little locomotives as they go busily about their work transporting tourists up to Blaenau Ffestiniog. Who could have imagined the change in use these little locos would go though. From being very industrial workhorses, built and maintained at nearby Boston Lodge from 1835 onwards, to being made redundant in 1946 and facing the junk yard cutting torches. Then onto being bought by volunteers in 1954 and the establishment of a trust set up to develop a successful tourist trade by 1981.

The footpath follows the edge of the bustling Porthmadog harbour, which was constructed in 1824. It really came into its own after the construction of the Ffestiniog railway, when it was used as a slate port and a centre of ship building in the area. At one time it could lay claim to the fact that over three hundred vessels were built in local yards. These vessels were to ply their trade all over the world, from Europe to the New World. Unfortunately it became clear that transportation by railway was much easier and the shipping trade declined. Over time the harbour and estuary started to silt up rendering an approach for cargo vessels difficult.

The path later emerges next to the picturesque bay of Borth y Gest. The shipbuilding, which had begun in Porthmadog, later moved to this bay. In the late 1800's shipbuilding locally reached its peak with the construction of the largest sailing ship to have been built in the area. It was the three-masted Barque "The Pride of Wales", 298 registered tons, 125ft in length, 26½ft beam and with a draught of 14½ft. Due to her size the local ship builders thought her owner/builder David Morris and her designer Simon Jones totally mad. They said the ship was too big to be launched in the waters off Borth y Gest, thankfully they were all proved wrong. She was successfully launched in 1868 and for nearly 25 strenuous years was to ply her trade over the world's oceans. She was to flounder in a great storm in the North Atlantic in 1892. At one time there were 8 shipyards between Porthmadog and Borth y Gest. Between 1826 and 1913, they were to build no fewer than 260 craft of between 30-40 tons.

As the walk climbs the flanks of Moel y Gest, the views are obscured by mixed woodlands. Later as the ridge is reached the views open up. The views extend to the mountains of Snowdonia and closer at hand the fairy tale Italianate village of Portmeirion built by Sir Clough Ellis Williams. Harlech castle built by Edward I in 1283 can be seen nestling under the Rhinog mountain range. To the right of Cardigan Bay can be seen Cricieth castle, erected by Llywelyn ap Iorwerth in the 13th century, later becoming the possession of Edward 1st who repaired and strengthened it. Further up the coast is the bustling yachting centre of Pwllheli. Below the flanks of Moel y Gest is the village of Penmorfa where a monument stands to Sir John Owen of Clenennau. Above the village of Tremadog are a series of igneous rock faces. They have become a Mecca for rock climbers particularly when the weather is poor in Snowdonia. Close by to Tremadog is the protected Coed Tremadog woodland with its rare ashwoods. The ridge terminates at an unexcavated fort.

The Walk: Depart from the Welsh Highland Railway Terminus or either car park and cross to the Ffestiniog Railway Station. Leave the station walking towards Porthmadog and cross the bridge. At the end of bridge L along sea wall passing the Tourist Information Centre and Harbour Master's Office on the R. Continue around the harbour to join road. Go along the road until a sign "Walkway to Borth y Gest" will be seen on the gable end of the yacht club building. Carry on passing boatyards on L. **1.** Carry on up footpath passing between properties. At junction go down road then down steps to beach. **2.** Cross the road and pass between houses "Borthwen" and "Isallt". Now along narrow path passing through gate into field. Keep on right-hand side of field to pass through a kissing gate and into woodland. Through next gate with white cottage on R. Go up lane passing "Tan y Coed" on L. On reaching road (which is in fact a lay by) go R to main road. Go R along road passing "Pen Aber" on R to just pass 30mph sign. **3.** At sign for "Tyddyn Llwyn" Camping site, cross road and take road for camping site (ignoring private road sign). Pass through camping site on tarmac road to where it dips and swings to the L. Here keep on across the site to the top LH corner (with climbing frame on the R). Now cross the stream and go through field gate. Path now climbs through ferns and later over a ladder stile. 25meters after next ladder stile path splits. **4.** Go sharp L uphill. The path soon emerges from the trees and crosses an old wall to continue climbing to follow another old wall on L. From here spectacular views of Cardigan Bay can be seen. Descend into a small col then easily scramble to the summit of Moel y Gest.

Unfortunately for the return to Porthmadog, the outward walk must be followed in reverse.

Refreshments: As well as the Ffestiniog Station restaurant there are a number of pubs and cafés in the area serving meals. Kerfoots near the roundabout on the High St is good for browsing and food.

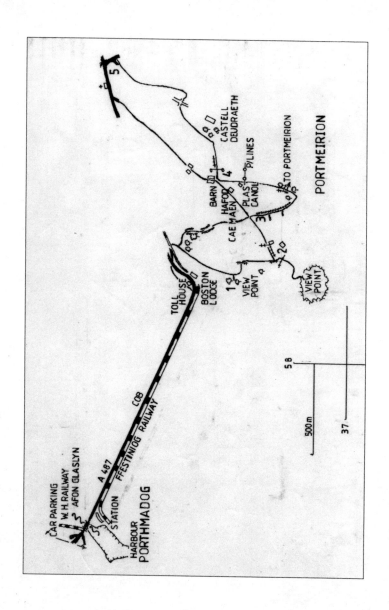

13. In Search of two most extraordinary Architects

Maps: 1:50,000 OS Landranger sheet 124 Porthmadog and Dolgellau or 1:25,000 OS Explorer sheet OL18 Harlech, Porthmadog and Y Bala.
Distance: 5½ Miles / 8.8 Kilometres.
Height gained: 165 ft/50 meters.
Duration: 3 Hours
Terrain: Paths are in woodland, open fields and lanes.
Stations/Halt: Porthmadog.
Car Park: Ffestiniog Narrow Gauge Railway Station also close by at grid reference SH569385 (pay and display).

In 1791 the Member of Parliament for Boston in Lincolnshire, William Alexander Madocks settled at Tan yr Allt close to what was to become the village of Tremadog. Being by nature an entrepreneur, the first of his many projects was to build and run a water powered woollen mill. This later became a laundry but unfortunately it later fell into dereliction and has recently been demolished. In 1800 he had started to reclaim some of the estuary near his home, which allowed him to venture into farming. During this period he realised that both agriculture and transport would benefit by reclaiming more of the estuary by building a barrage across its mouth. He was oblivious to the fact that such an action would result in the loss of the fishing fleet located further up river at the mouth of the Aberglaslyn gorge.

In 1807 he commenced what must have appeared to most a very foolhardy project. By 1811 "The Cob" had not only been completed but had been opened to traffic. All for the cost in those days of £160,000. His success was to be short lived when the embankment was breached in a fierce gale. The locals, who must have believed in Madocks and his project, rallied around to collect funds to enable repairs to be carried out.

Since 1811 there has been a tollhouse at the Boston Lodge end of the Cob and a toll for this crossing was fixed by an act of parliament. This operated until 28th April 1978, when it was taken over by the Rebecca Trust who charged 5 pence for the privilege of crossing the Cob. It was also the cause of long and frustrating delays for the motorist. Money collected by the Rebecca Trust was given to local charities. At 09.15 on Friday 28th March 2003 the toll charge was taken away for good.

After the completion of the embankment Madocks continued to find new projects to keep him occupied; one such project being the construction of a harbour. This was to become Porthmadog and was completed in 1824. Almost at once, this started to serve the mines and quarries in the area, which were looking for the means to transport their goods to markets. In 1836, a narrow gauge railway line was constructed across the embankment to enable slate to be brought from the Ffestiniog quarries to the port. This in turn led to the construction locally of purpose designed Schooners, which were built and sailed from this quiet corner of Wales to ports all around the globe. These Schooners were affectionately known as Western Ocean Racers. They had sleek bows and sterns yet sported a bulbous amidships for maximum cargo carrying capacity.

Unfortunately due to the decline of the slate industry the Ffestiniog railway closed in 1946 and faced dereliction and the scrap mans blowtorch. With no prospect of the industry starting up again the railway faced certain closure. Fortunately in 1954 volunteers set up a trust to purchase the line and the remains of the rolling stock.

In 1955 track repairs were under way and Boston Lodge Foundry was refurbished to commence the difficult renovation of those beautiful locomotives, which can be seen today. On the 24th May 1982 after many setbacks the line was re-opened to Blaenau Ffestiniog for the tourist trade.

The estuary is now a haven for bird watchers, especially with the return of the Ospreys to the area around Pont Croesor. Otter sightings have been reported close to the harbour in recent years.

The other well-known architect in the area is Sir Clough Williams-Ellis. Known primarily for the Italianate village of Portmeirion, he was also the designer of the original café on Snowdon's summit. Clough Williams-Ellis was born in 1893 into a distinguished Welsh family. From an early age he described the Welsh landscape as very dull and spartan and so to find solace in his lonely rural life he designed and constructed model buildings with basically anything he could lay his hands on. He studied Natural Science at Cambridge, later moving to London where he was to continue his studies under the guidance of his uncle, the Lord Lieutenant of Meirionnydd. It was his uncle who appointed the young Clough to become magistrate of that county, a position he was never to take up. Architecture was to dominate Clough's life, even though it could have been classed as eccentric. He was to design anything from cottages to war memorials, schools to churches; he even designed an upright grand piano. The completed object must have appeared monstrous and probably sounded worse.

It was to be Portmeirion that became Clough's claim to fame. The idea of the Italianate village came to him after his visit to Sorrento in Italy. After spending a number of years searching for a suitable location in such far away places as New Zealand, he was to eventually purchase land five miles from his home at Brondanw. The land, known as "Aber Iâ" (frozen river mouth) was owned by a relative of his, Sir Osmond Williams and was tenanted by a recluse, Miss Adelaide Haig. She had let the land become overgrown and neglected in order to keep visitors at bay but for Clough, this was just what he wanted. From 1925 for the next 50 years he cleared the land and in the process purchased adjoining properties. He returned the mansion house to its former glory and opened it as a hotel, fortunately many of his guests were friends who never complained or were perhaps too polite to complain about the lack of electric and appalling food. The fact that neither Clough nor his staff knew anything about running a hotel and cheerfully acknowledged this fact did little to improve matters. The hotel was sadly gutted by fire in 1981, but with his typical love and devotion to his buildings he began a seven-year restoration project that would restore it to its former glory.

Clough was to buy up all types of derelict buildings and items from all over the world. He would move them to his project at Portmeirion but was to insist that no more than two buildings were of the same style. His Town Hall with its Jacobean ceiling, panelling and mullion windows were saved at the last minute from Emerald Hall in Flintshire. This provided the hall with excellent acoustics in which such musicians as Sir Arthur Bliss, Gerald Moore and Yvonne Arnaud have performed. The bandstand was an electricity substation and some of the paving slabs were the blanks cut out from slate lavatory seats. Even a statue of Hercules with a 1959 inscription on the base now stands majestically outside the Hercules Hall.

A number of notable people were to stay at Portmeirion. Noel Coward was to write "Blithe Spirit" in the fountain, George Bernard Shaw was to visit and one distinguished guest insisted he brought his entourage of "Bunny Girls" with him. It was thought to have been the location of Wing Commander Guy Gibson's last leave before he flew on the "Dam Buster" mission. The catalyst that brought Portmeirion to the attention of the general public was the 1960's cult TV series "The Prisoner" starring Patrick McGoohan. Clough decided to name his project Portmeirion because he considered it to be the Port of Meirionnydd. However, the only resemblance to a port in this brightly pastel coloured village is the concrete half boat constructed into the sea wall.

Clough received a Knighthood in 1972. He lived in nearby Brondanw with his wife Annabel Strachey, daughter of John St Loe Strachey, the Editor of "The Spectator". The house with its magnificent gardens is now looked after by his daughter. Clough died in 1973 at the age of 93. As is the way with many eccentrics, he wanted to mark his passing with a spectacular ending. He wanted to have his ashes packed into a firework rocket and fired over Portmeirion scattering his ashes in a most spectacular fashion. Sad to say his widow thought this was inappropriate and it's thought that his ashes were scattered in a much less spectacular manner.

Portmeirion is now looked after by a limited company and receives about 240,000 visitors per annum. The gardens at Brondanw are also open the public for all to enjoy.

The Walk: Start from the Ffestiniog Narrow Gauge Railway Station and head out along the Cob keeping railway on R. At end of Cob, close to engineering works (Boston Lodge) the path descends steps to the main road. Cross this and on to Cycle route. Now go R passing old toll house and to far end of lay by. Cross main road and up track (marked with a bridle way sign) to station (Boston Lodge halt). Cross over railway line and follow footpath through gate and into woods, with wall on L. **1.** At fork go R following narrow grassy path passing through gate and up to a vantage point. From here there are spectacular views of Porthmadog, the estuary and also the surrounding mountains. Continue along path to pass through gate into field. Now go R along vague path (with fence on R) to pass through fence gap (gateway) close to farm. **2.** Go R through small gate. Now ½ R up to viewpoint. Return to small gate and go L through fence gap (gateway), then R crossing field with fence and buildings on R to two gates. Through the R/H gate and along track. **3.** At track junction (cattle grid in front) R down grassy path passing through gaps in two high walls and down to gate. Path now descends between wall and fence until the Portmeirion boundary is reached. L up path following footpath signs to gate with stile. Zig zag to R (this is the access to the Portmeirion entry kiosk and car park) Over stile and up field keeping as close as possible to L/H boundary passing under power lines. Through gate to join lane (Plas Canol on L). **4.** At track junction, immediately before barn go R into field, path follows L/H field boundary (from this position more spectacular mountain scenery comes into view). Through gate and into woods, continuing with fence on L. Cross road and down lane passing bungalow on R. At T- junction, go L along lane and down to road (signs for Maes y Garth and Cae Eithin). L to main road. **5.** L along main road to pass chapel and house Moel y Ddol on R. 75 meters after these properties L up lane. At track junction take L/H fork to pass between houses and along to farmyard. Over cattle grid (same as location **4.**) and take R fork uphill. At Hafod Cae Maen continue to cattle grid (same as location **3.**). Go R along track, which ascends for a short distance then descends between walls. When track swings sharp R and levels out, continue on through gate and down grassy path into woodland. Descend to Boston Lodge Halt. From here descend to cross the main road to join the cycle path. Continue along the cycle path (not the railway track) back into Porthmadog. On this return section you may be able to view the bird life in the area. You may perhaps be fortunate enough to see the otters reputed to have returned to the area.

Refreshments: As well as the Ffestiniog Station restaurant there are a number of pubs and cafés in the area serving meals. At the north end of Snowdon Street is the famous fish and chip shop "Allports".

Entrance fees in 2009 for Portmeirion were £7.50 for adults. Contact them on 01766 772311 for opening hours.

14. Nantmor to Porthmadog by way of Traeth Mawr

When we were planning the book we always envisaged having a low level walk between Nantmor and Porthmadog. There were public rights of way, which made this seem feasible, but when we eventually came around to walking the route our plan fell apart. One particular section went beyond what we could expect people to pass through and so we decided not to include it in the same way as the other routes. If weather and ground conditions allow it may be possible but at the time we attempted it, the only way it could have been completed would have been in waders and snorkel. So we have included this walk, although with no instructions, to allow you to make your own decision whether to continue this walk.

On initial exploration the walk was thought to be an enjoyable and easy excursion for when the weather was against exploring any of the high level walks. Unfortunately where the well marked footpath had to pass to the rear of the farm Ty'n y Celyn (grid reference SH598421), it was found to be impassable and from there on to join Pont Croesor was most unpleasant. The footpath shown on the Ordnance Survey map slightly to the east of this route no longer exists. Therefore the only time this footpath would be suitable would be during the height of summer when the area has dried out, and then most walkers would wish to be on the high tops.

The walk departs from the request halt at Nantmor. Nantmor appears to be a corruption of Nant y Môr which means stream by the sea. At one time prior to the area being reclaimed the sea did extend as far as the Aberglaslyn Bridge, the pool Llyn Glas and the fishing village of Aber, of which very little remains. In 1625, Sir John Wynn of Gwydir contacted his cousin who was a civil engineer with experience of land reclamation. However due to the costs involved, no attempt was made to reclaim the land in this area. It wasn't until the 1800's when William Madocks became involved, that the estuary was reclaimed.

The hamlet of Nantmor has been renowned for its poets. Rhys Goch Eryri (Red Rhys of Snowdon) lived here during his life (1385-1448). He was described by George Borrow as a poet and partisan of Owain Glyndŵr. Rhys Goch helped Owain Glyndŵr escape from the clutches of Henry 5th's forces. Rhys Goch's home Hafod Garegog lies along the route and has been extensively renovated over the years. Rhys Goch was to teach the poet Dafydd Nantmor (1410-1480). He in turn was to teach poet Rhys Nantmor. Dafydd Nantmor was banished from the area and lived in exile in South Wales after he wrote and sung a poem to a married woman, Gwen o'r Ddôl.

Walkers familiar with the area in the 1980's may have, with some surprise, noticed sheep with long necks. On closer examination they would have turned out to be Lamas owned by Ruth Jannette Ruck. She published a number of books about her experiences on running a Welsh hill farm and owning Lamas. In 1980 she was featured on the HTV series "About Britain" as the "Lady and the Lamas".

The path passes very close to the nesting site of the "Glaslyn Ospreys". These birds have, much to the delight of enthusiastic bird watchers, been coming to this area since 2004. The RSPB hide close to the Croesor Bridge can be visited between March and September. With the use of high-powered binoculars it is possible to see the nesting pairs of Ospreys.

From Pren-teg the footpath follows the railway line into Porthmadog. Whilst walking through the industrial site the road crosses over what appears to be a drainage ditch. This is in fact the remains of the canal called the "Tremadog Canal" or "Y Cyt" constructed by William Madocks to add prestige to Tremadog. It was capable of accommodating vessels of sea going size, which imported coal and other commodities such as wool.

The Walk: Departs the request halt (check to see that it has been completed otherwise use the Fisherman's path as a link from Beddgelert) and climbs through the hamlet of Nantmor along the narrow road to a "T" junction. Here it joins the road from Llyn Dinas. Now go R to the junction with the A 4085. Cross this and follow the lane marked as a bridle way to pass Hafod Garegog on the R. Pass over the footbridge over Afon Dylif and up to an embankment. Here go R. The path now follows the embankment passing to the R of a barn and, further on, to the right of the farm of Ty'n y Celyn. Unfortunately from here to Pont Croesor, which can be seen a short distance away, is problematic due to the combination of deep mud and slurry. Even after a long period of dry weather it is uncertain if this area would dry out.

On joining the B4410, go R and cross the Croesor Bridge over Afon Glaslyn. At this location, during the summer period, it's well worth visiting the RSPB. Osprey Project. Follow the road up to the "T" junction with the A 498. Here go L to buildings on the L and join footpath passing close to these. The footpath now follows field boundaries to the railway line. The footpath runs alongside the line to a crossing close to the sports field L. Here, pass the sports field and along the road passing through the industrial site. Go over "Y Cyt" and the main line railway line into Porthmadog. Continue on, passing through a car park. Here it is possible to cross the line into a picnic area. The footpath follows the railway line crossing the main road and into the Ffestiniog Railway Station.

Further enjoyable reading on Snowdonia

Visit our website for further information:
www.carreg-gwalch.com

Orders can be placed on our
On-line Shop

More Walking Books ....

Visit our website for further information:
www.carreg-gwalch.com

Orders can be placed on our
On-line Shop

Also of interest ....

Visit our website for further information:
www.carreg-gwalch.com

Orders can be placed on our
On-line Shop